BLACK AMERICAN PROSE WRITERS
BEFORE THE HARLEM RENAISSANCE

Writers of English: Lives and Works

BLACK AMERICAN PROSE WRITERS

BEFORE THE HARLEM RENAISSANCE

Edited and with an Introduction by

Harold Bloom

CHELSEA HOUSE PUBLISHERS
New York   Philadelphia

Jacket illustration: **Egypt and Spring** by Laura Wheeler, cover design for *The Crisis*, April 1923 (edited by W. E. B. Du Bois) (courtesy of The Schomburg Center for Research in Black Culture, The New York Public Library, Astor, Lenox and Tilden Foundations).

CHELSEA HOUSE PUBLISHERS

Editorial Director Richard Rennert
Executive Managing Editor Karyn Gullen Browne
Executive Editor Sean Dolan
Copy Chief Robin James
Picture Editor Adrian G. Allen
Art Director Robert Mitchell
Manufacturing Director Gerald Levine
Production Coordinator Marie Claire Cebrián-Ume

Writers of English: Lives and Works

Senior Editor S. T. Joshi
Series Design Rae Grant

Staff for BLACK AMERICAN PROSE WRITERS BEFORE THE HARLEM RENAISSANCE

Researcher Richard Fumosa
Editorial Assistants Robert Green, Mary Sisson
Picture Researcher Wendy Wills

© 1994 by Chelsea House Publishers, a division of Main Line Book Co.

Introduction © 1994 by Harold Bloom

Printed and bound in the United States of America.

First Printing

1 3 5 7 9 8 6 4 2

Library of Congress Cataloging-in-Publication Data

Black American prose writers before the Harlem renaissance / edited and with an introduction by Harold Bloom.
    p. cm.—(Writers of English)
    ISBN 0-7910-2202-1.—ISBN 0-7910-2227-7 (pbk.)
    1. American prose literature—Afro-American authors—Bio-bibliography. 2. American prose literature—Afro-American authors—Dictionaries. 3. Afro-Americans—Intellectual life—Dictionaries. 4. Afro-Americans in literature—Bibliography. 5. Harlem Renaissance—Dictionaries. I. Bloom, Harold. II. Series.
PS366.A35B57 1994   93-13022
818′.50809896073—dc20   CIP

Contents

◈ User's Guide

THIS VOLUME PROVIDES biographical, critical, and bibliographical information on the thirteen most significant black American prose writers before the Harlem Renaissance. Each chapter consists of three parts: a biography of the author; a selection of brief critical extracts about the author; and a bibliography of the author's published books.

The biography supplies a detailed outline of the important events in the author's life, including his or her major writings. The critical extracts are taken from a wide array of books and periodicals, from the author's lifetime to the present, and range in content from biographical to critical to historical. The extracts are arranged in chronological order by date of writing or publication, and a full bibliographical citation is provided at the end of each extract. Editorial additions or deletions are indicated within carets.

The author bibliographies list every separate publication—including books, pamphlets, broadsides, collaborations, and works edited or translated by the author—for works published in the author's lifetime; selected important posthumous publications are also listed. Titles are those of the first edition; if a work has subsequently come to be known under a variant title, this title is supplied within carets. In selected instances dates of revised editions are given where these are significant. Pseudonymous works are listed but not the pseudonyms under which these works were published. Periodicals edited by the author are listed only when the author has written most or all of the contents. For plays we have listed date of publication, not date of production; unpublished plays are not listed. Titles enclosed in square brackets are of doubtful authenticity. All works by the author, whether in English or in other languages, have been listed; English translations of foreign-language works are not listed unless the author has done the translation.

The Life of the Author
Harold Bloom

NIETZSCHE, WITH EXULTANT ANGUISH, famously proclaimed that God was dead. Whatever the consequences of this for the ethical life, its ultimate literary effect certainly would have surprised the author Nietzsche. His French disciples, Foucault most prominent among them, developed the Nietzschean proclamation into the dogma that all authors, God included, were dead. The death of the author, which is no more than a Parisian trope, another metaphor for fashion's setting of skirt-lengths, is now accepted as literal truth by most of our current apostles of what should be called French Nietzsche, to distinguish it from the merely original Nietzsche. We also have French Freud or Lacan, which has little to do with the actual thought of Sigmund Freud, and even French Joyce, which interprets *Finnegans Wake* as the major work of Jacques Derrida. But all this is as nothing compared to the final triumph of the doctrine of the death of the author: French Shakespeare. That delicious absurdity is given us by the New Historicism, which blends Foucault and California fruit juice to give us the Word that Renaissance "social energies," and not William Shakespeare, composed *Hamlet* and *King Lear*. It seems a proper moment to murmur "enough" and to return to a study of the life of the author.

Sometimes it troubles me that there are so few masterpieces in the vast ocean of literary biography that stretches between James Boswell's great *Life* of Dr. Samuel Johnson and the late Richard Ellmann's wonderful *Oscar Wilde*. Literary biography is a crucial genre, and clearly a difficult one in which to excel. The actual nature of the lives of the poets seems to have little effect upon the quality of their biographies. Everything happened to Lord Byron and nothing at all to Wallace Stevens, and yet their biographers seem equally daunted by them. But even inadequate biographies of strong writers, or of weak ones, are of immense use. I have never read a literary biography from which I have not profited, a statement I cannot make about any other genre whatsoever. And when it comes to figures who are central to us—Dante, Shakespeare, Cervantes, Montaigne, Goethe, Whitman, Tolstoi, Freud, Joyce, Kafka among them—we reach out eagerly for every scrap that the biographers have gleaned. Concerning Dante and Shakespeare we know much too little, yet when we come to Goethe and Freud, where we seem to know more than everything, we still want to know more. The death of the author, despite our current resentniks, clearly was only a momentary fad. Something vital in every authentic lover of literature responds to Emerson's battle-cry sentence: "There is no history, only biography." Beyond that there is a deeper truth, difficult to come at and requiring a lifetime to understand, which is that there is no literature, only autobiography, however mediated, however veiled, however transformed. The events of Shakespeare's life included the composition of *Hamlet,* and that act of writing was itself a crucial act of living, though we do not yet know altogether how to read so doubled an act. When an author takes up a more overtly autobiographical stance, as so many do in their youth, again we still do not know precisely how to accommodate the vexed relation between life and work. T. S. Eliot, meditating upon James Joyce, made a classic statement as to such accommodation:

> We want to know who are the originals of his characters, and what
> were the origins of his episodes, so that we may unravel the web of memory
> and invention and discover how far and in what ways the crude material
> has been transformed.

When a writer is not even covertly autobiographical, the web of memory and invention is still there, but so subtly woven that we may never unravel it. And yet we want deeply never to stop trying, and not merely because we are curious, but because each of us is caught in her own network of memory and invention. We do not always recall our inventions, and long before we age we cease to be certain of the extent to which we have invented our memories. Perhaps one motive for reading is our need to unravel our own webs. If our masters could make, from their lives, what we read, then we can be moved by them to ask: What have we made or lived in relation to what we have read? The answers may be sad, or confused, but the question is likely, implicitly, to go on being asked as long as we read. In Freudian terms, we are asking: What is it that we have repressed? What have we forgotten, unconsciously but purposively: What is it that we flee? Art, literature necessarily included, is regression in the service of the ego, according to a famous Freudian formula. I doubt the Freudian wisdom here, but indubitably it is profoundly suggestive. When we read, something in us keeps asking the equivalent of the Freudian questions: From what or whom is the author in flight, and to what earlier stages in her life is she returning, and why?

Reading, whether as an art or a pastime, has been damaged by the visual media, television in particular, and might be in some danger of extinction in the age of the computer, except that the psychic need for it continues to endure, presumably because it alone can assuage a central loneliness in elitist society. Despite all sophisticated or resentful denials, the reading of imaginative literature remains a quest to overcome the isolation of the individual consciousness. We can read for information, or entertainment, or for love of the language, but in the end we seek, in the author, the person whom we have not found, whether in ourselves or in others. In that quest, there always are elements at once aggressive and defensive, so that reading, even in childhood, is rarely free of hidden anxieties. And yet it remains one of the few activities not contaminated by an entropy of spirit. We read in hope, because we lack companionship, and the author can become the object of the most idealistic elements in our search for the wit and inventiveness we so desperately require. We read biography, not as a supplement to reading the author, but as a second, fresh attempt to understand what always seems to evade us in the work, our drive towards a kind of identity with the author.

This will-to-identity, though recently much deprecated, is a prime basis for the experience of sublimity in reading. *Hamlet* retains its unique position in the Western canon not because most readers and playgoers identify themselves with the prince, who clearly is beyond them, but rather because they find themselves again in the power of the language that represents him with such immediacy and force. Yet we know that neither language nor social energy created Hamlet. Our curiosity about Shakespeare is endless, and never will be appeased. That curiosity itself is a value, and cannot be separated from the value of *Hamlet* the tragedy, or Hamlet the literary character. It provokes us that Shakespeare the man seems so unknowable, at once everyone and no one as Borges shrewdly observes. Critics keep telling us otherwise, yet something valid in us keeps believing that we would know Hamlet better if Shakespeare's life were as fully known as the lives of Goethe and Freud, Byron and Oscar Wilde, or best of all, Dr. Samuel Johnson. Shakespeare never will have his Boswell, and Dante never will have his Richard Ellmann. How much one would give for a detailed and candid *Life of Dante* by Petrarch, or an outspoken memoir of Shakespeare by Ben Jonson! Or, in the age just past, how superb would be rival studies of one another by Hemingway and Scott Fitzgerald! But the list is endless: think of *Oscar Wilde* by Lord Alfred Douglas, or a joint biography of Shelley by Mary Godwin, Emilia Viviani, and Jane Williams. More than our insatiable desire for scandal would be satisfied. The literary rivals and the lovers of the great writers possessed perspectives we will never enjoy, and without those perspectives we dwell in some poverty in regard to the writers with whom we ourselves never can be done.

There is a sense in which imaginative literature *is* perspectivism, so that the reader is likely to be overwhelmed by the work's difficulty unless its multiple perspectives are mastered. Literary biography matters most because it is a storehouse of perspectives, frequently far surpassing any that are grasped by the particular biographer. There are relations between authors' lives and their works of kinds we have yet to discover, because our analytical instruments are not yet advanced enough to perform the necessary labor. Perhaps a novel, poem, or play is not so much a regression in the service of the ego, as it is an amalgam of *all* the Freudian mechanisms of defense, all working together for the apotheosis of the ego. Freud valued art highly, but thought that the aesthetic enterprise was no rival for psychoanalysis, unlike religion and philosophy. Clearly Freud was mistaken; his own anxieties about his indebtedness to Shakespeare helped produce the weirdness of his joining in the lunacy that argued for the Earl of Oxford as the author of

Shakespeare's plays. It was Shakespeare, and not "the poets," who was there before Freud arrived at his depth psychology, and it is Shakespeare who is there still, well out ahead of psychoanalysis. We see what Freud would not see, that psychoanalysis is Shakespeare prosified and systematized. Freud is part of literature, not of "science," and the biography of Freud has the same relations to psychoanalysis as the biography of Shakespeare has to *Hamlet* and *King Lear*, if only we knew more of the life of Shakespeare.

Western literature, particularly since Shakespeare, is marked by the representation of internalized change in its characters. A literature of the ever-growing inner self is in itself a large form of biography, even though this is the biography of imaginary beings, from Hamlet to the sometimes nameless protagonists of Kafka and Beckett. Skeptics might want to argue that all literary biography concerns imaginary beings, since authors make themselves up, and every biographer gives us a creation curiously different from the same author as seen by the writer of a rival *Life*. Boswell's Johnson is not quite anyone else's Johnson, though it is now very difficult for us to disentangle the great Doctor from his gifted Scottish friend and follower. The life of the author is not merely a metaphor or a fiction, as is "the Death of the Author," but it always does contain metaphorical or fictive elements. Those elements are a part of the value of literary biography, but not the largest or the crucial part, which is the separation of the mask from the man or woman who hid behind it. James Joyce and Samuel Beckett, master and sometime disciple, were both of them enigmatic personalities, and their biographers have not, as yet, fully expounded the mystery of these contrasting natures. Beckett seems very nearly to have been a secular saint: personally disinterested, heroic in the French Resistance, as humane a person ever to have composed major fictions and dramas. Joyce, self-obsessed even as Beckett was preternaturally selfless, was the Milton of the twentieth century. Beckett was perhaps the least egoistic post-Joycean, post-Proustian, post-Kafkan of writers. Does that illuminate the problematical nature of his work, or does it simply constitute another problem? Whatever the cause, the question matters. The only death of the author that is other than literal, and that matters, is the fate only of weak writers. The strong, who become canonical, never die, which is what the canon truly is about. To be read forever is the Life of the Author.

▨ *Introduction*

THE SLAVE NARRATIVE and the African-American sermon, as two among the crucial kinds of earlier African-American writing, made it inevitable that criticism of such writing should seek biography as one of its foundations. Frederick Douglass's *Narrative* of his life retains considerable literary strength as an autobiographical fragment, but its largest value may be that it holds itself open to be completed by its readers and inheritors. Robert G. O'Meally has argued persuasively that "the text was meant to be preached" as a black sermon calling upon blacks and whites to rise up together against the sadism of slavery. Complex as Douglass's religious stance was, its prophetic burden is clear. In the best sense, all nineteenth- and early twentieth-century African-American writing has a religious and moral design upon us. Tendentious writing, in a religious context, is the norm, and the American Religion, our still-developing national mixture of ancient gnosis, eighteenth-century Enthusiasm, and nineteenth-century Orphism, always has relied upon African-American religion as its hidden paradigm. One of the major ironies of American history is that the Southern Baptist Convention, which has become the Catholic church of the South, as Martin Marty observes, takes its spiritual origin, quite unknowingly, from the early black Baptists in America. The gnosis of "the little me within the big me," an African religious inheritance, has become the characteristic American sense of a spirit that is no part of the creation, and that goes back to before the foundation of the world.

Robert B. Stepto eloquently emphasized that "finding a voice" is Douglass's ultimate image, and his principal legacy. That voice, in Houston A. Baker, Jr.'s view, falls away in Douglass's revisions, partly because Douglass too naively identified liberation with literacy. Both scholars seem accurate in these perceptions, and their apparent disagreement may be only dialectical, even if the synthesis is not available as yet in African-American studies. Such a synthesis, if and when it is accomplished, will require more understanding than is now available as to just what are the full relations between a writer's life and the work that he composes. Where spirituality becomes the middle term that intervenes between the chronical of a life and the history of a text, then our need for biographical criticism and speculation becomes all the greater.

Ann Kibbey has demonstrated that Frederick Douglass broke both with American Protestantism, compromised as it was by its alliance with the slave system, and also with the symbolism and rhetoric of Christian narrative. Douglass's rejection of such Christian literary forms may be more important than his actual literary and social achievement, since it is difficult not to feel that Douglass was a prophet, both voluntary and involuntary. Writing about Douglass and most other early African-American authors has a tendency to become a workshop for fresh theories as to the nature of more recent African-American literary achievement, if only because Douglass was more revolutionary than he knew. Since so much African-American literature remains overtly autobiographical, critic and biographer tend to fuse, as they so frequently do in the criticism of autobiography. The late Michael Cooke, studying African-American autobiography, subtly saw the genre's coordinates as being "the self as content" and "the self as shaped." Literary biography and biographical criticism, the study of the life of the author, perpetually seeks to reconcile the two coordinates, and never more urgently than in the investigation and appreciation of African-American literature.

—H. B.

William Stanley Braithwaite
1878–1962

WILLIAM STANLEY BRAITHWAITE was born in Boston on December 26, 1878, the son of Emma De Wolfe and William Smith Braithwaite. His father, who was from a distinguished West Indian family, educated the Braithwaite children in the genteel atmosphere of their home. Upon the death of the elder Braithwaite, William Stanley, now in his eighth year, began to attend school. His formal education came to an end four years later when his desire to help support his family led to an apprenticeship at Ginn & Company, where he was exposed to the world of books. Braithwaite made frequent trips to the Boston Public Library to educate himself.

In June 1903 Braithwaite married Emma Kelly, with whom he had seven children. His first volume of poetry, *Lyrics of Life and Love*, was published in 1904 and reflected the influence of the English Romantic poets, especially Keats and Shelley. Although Braithwaite favorably reviewed many poets who used nontraditional poetic language and devices, his own poetry was, for the most part, marked by technical precision and recognizable literary influences. His poems continued to be published in magazines and journals such as *New England Magazine*, *American Magazine*, *Voice*, *Century*, *Atlantic Monthly*, and *Book News Monthly*. In 1908 his second collection of verse, *The House of Falling Leaves*, was published. The volume showed an increasing attraction toward the sonnet as well as a tendency toward mysticism— possibly a reflection of Braithwaite's interest in William Blake—and included many pieces in celebration of particular persons. Though he was not insensitive to the plight of fellow black American writers, Braithwaite's early poetry was not influenced by, or concerned with, issues of race.

The depth of Braithwaite's interest in poetry was manifested in his emergence as a leading critic of verse. The influence of his columns in the *Boston Transcript*, articles in black periodicals, and the appearance of his *Poetry Journal* in 1912 (a short-lived enterprise that lasted only until 1914) inspired W. E. B. Du Bois to call Braithwaite "the most prominent critic of poetry in America." Braithwaite did much to foster new American poets, especially those of African-American heritage, and it became a coveted honor to have poems reviewed by him and included in his yearly anthologies, the first of which was the *Anthology of Magazine Verse for 1913*. The annual anthologies of American verse continued to appear until 1929. He also published *The Book of Elizabethan Verse* (1908), *The Book of Georgian Verse* (1909), *The Book of Restoration Verse* (1910), and *Our Lady's Choir: A Contemporary Anthology of Verse by Catholic Sisters* (1931). Though Braithwaite's stature as an eminent critic of American poetry continued to grow, he never lost interest in British literature, which influenced his early writings. In 1919 he edited *The Book of Modern British Verse*, and in 1950 *The Bewitched Parsonage: The Story of the Brontës* appeared.

In 1935 Braithwaite, relinquishing his seat in Boston society, accepted the position of professor of creative literature at Atlanta University, where he remained for ten years. Despite his prestigious position in the world of letters, Braithwaite was painfully aware of his lack of formal education in the academic surroundings. It should not be surprising that he remained aloof from the politics of academia, never wavering in his devotion to his students. Braithwaite retired from Atlanta University in 1945 and moved to Harlem. His *Selected Poems* appeared in 1948, and he continued to write for various periodicals. He died on June 8, 1962.

Critical Extracts

BENJAMIN BRAWLEY   Very recently (1917) Mr. Braithwaite has brought together in a volume, *The Poetic Year*, the series of articles which he contributed to the *Transcript* in 1916–17. The aim was in the form of conversations between a small group of friends to discuss the poetry of 1916. Says he: "There were four of us in the little group, and our common love for the art of poetry suggested a weekly meeting in the grove to discuss the books we had all agreed upon reading. . . . I made up my mind to record these discussions, and the setting as well, with all those other touches of human character and mood which never fail to enliven and give color to the serious business of art and life. . . . I gave fanciful names to my companions, Greek names which I am persuaded symbolized the spirit of each. There was nothing Psyche touched but made its soul apparent. Her wood-lore was beautiful and thorough; the very spirit of flowers, birds and trees was evoked when she went among them. Our other companion of her sex was Cassandra, and we gave her this name not because her forebodings were gloomy, but merely for her prophesying disposition, which was always building air-castles. The other member besides myself of our little group was Jason, of the heroic dreams and adventuresome spirit. He was restless in the bonds of a tranquillity that chafed the hidden spirit of his being." From the introduction we get something of the critic's own aims and ideals: "The conversational scheme of the book may, or may not, interest some readers. Poetry is a human thing, and it is time for the world—and especially our part of the world—to regard it as belonging to people. It sprang from the folk, and passed, when culture began to flourish, into the possession of a class. Now culture is passing from a class to the folk, and with it poetry is returning to its original possessors. It is in the spirit of these words that we discuss the poetry of the year." Emphasis is here given to this work because it is the sturdiest achievement of Mr. Braithwaite in the field in which he has recently become most distinguished, and even the brief quotations cited are sufficient to give some idea of his graceful, suggestive prose.

Benjamin Brawley, *The Negro in Literature and Art in the United States* (NY: Duffield, 1921), pp. 57–59.

PHILIP BUTCHER   Recalling his years as a member of the English faculty at Atlanta University, William Stanley Braithwaite thought some of his colleagues "rather offish" and quite degree conscious.

> Always in an institution of that sort your colleagues are interested
> to know where you got your education and where you got
> your degrees, and I told them frankly I had no earned degrees,
> not even a high school diploma. I don't know just what they
> thought, but sometimes their action was a puzzlement. They had
> a conference there of English teachers from Negro colleges.
> I'm not much for conferences. The man who was the head of
> the English Department at Morehouse College, Nathaniel
> P. Tillman, invited me to become a member, and I said, "I don't
> want to become a member."

⟨. . .⟩ He said that once he refused the command of his department chairman that he attend a staff meeting to prepare an examination on the fundamentals, reminding her that he had come to the university in 1935 to teach literature to English majors and to direct the research of graduate students. He was not insensitive to the plight of students who had cultural deprivation; he had a strong commitment to and rapport with those youths who heard his occasional chapel lectures as well as with the select few who were enrolled in his advanced courses. But he felt the need to reserve his energies for the specific tasks he had undertaken. And he had a sense of special vulnerability as an intruder from the non-academic world, unsupported by the conventional credentials of the profession. During his early months on the faculty he could not quite understand what seemed to him a lack of cordiality, and it was not until a year or two had passed that he learned the aloofness he detected was due to his colleagues' respect for his status in the world of letters rather than to scorn for the inadequacies of his formal training.

He was "Dr. Braithwaite" on campus by virtue of an honorary Doctor of Literature degree granted by Talladega College in 1918; Atlanta had given him an honorary M.A. in the same year. As testimonials to his learning these awards were superfluous. Though his poetry seems now of minor significance, his attainments as critic, editor, and anthologist add up to genuine distinction. Since 1906 his reviews and articles in the Boston *Transcript* had made him a literary figure of national importance, one of the best informed and most influential critics of poetry in America. His period anthologies of English poetry, beginning with *The Book of Elizabethan Verse* in 1906, and the seventeen annual collections of the best American magazine verse he compiled until the Depression put an end to the series were standards of their kind. As president of the B. J. Brimmer Company he published such works as the first novel of James Gould Cozzens and Georgia Douglas Johnson's *Bronze*. His extraordinarily wide acquaintance with poets, editors, novelists, publishers, and literary notables of all sorts is attested by the hundreds of pieces of correspondence in the Braithwaite Papers that Harvard University acquired for its library at Depression rates. If Braithwaite was short on academic credentials, there was no question whatever about his real qualifications as a teacher. Nor was there doubt about his devotion to the youngsters he exerted himself to know both as students and people. To them, to his colleagues, and to skeptical administrators he reiterated one conviction: a lack of background—of formal educational training or personal cultural advantages—need not prevent intellectual or artistic achievement. He had his own career as irrefutable evidence of the validity of his doctrine.

Philip Butcher, "William Stanley Braithwaite and the College Language Association," *CLA Journal* 15, No. 2 (December 1971): 117–20

PHILIP BUTCHER   Writing in praise of William Stanley Braithwaite, awarded the 1918 Spingarn Medal as "the American citizen of African
descent who made last year the highest achievement in any field of elevated
human endeavor," W. E. B. Du Bois called him "the most prominent critic
of poetry in America." So influential was Braithwaite at the time that a
celebrated rival, Harriet Monroe, dubbed him "Sir Oracle" and "the Boston
dictator." Poets as notable as Robert Frost and Amy Lowell courted his
favor, as did Claude McKay and Countee Cullen. William Dean Howells,
who spoke with the highest authority, once said Braithwaite was "the most
intellectual historian of contemporary poetry I know." Yet this poet, critic,
editor, anthologist, and publisher, whose books fill a whole shelf, has been
ignored or slighted in most textbooks and histories of American literature
as a whole, and even in the current flood of anthologies and studies of "the
black experience" he has received less recognition than his labors and
accomplishments merit. ⟨. . .⟩

On February 14, 1906, Braithwaite began to contribute to the Boston
Evening Transcript, a newspaper that enjoyed at that time a status not unlike
that of today's *New York Times*. The reviews and essays he published in its
pages were a major source of income for him for twenty years, though he
was never a salaried staff member. They constituted the bulk of his critical
writing and the principal basis for his authority in the world of letters.
Through them, he labored to enlarge the audience for verse, encourage and
assist fledgling poets, and win for talent and genius appropriate recognition.
He became a significant force in revitalizing poetry in America.

One outgrowth of his work with the *Transcript* was his publication of a
slender *Anthology of Magazine Verse for 1913*. For the next sixteen years he
issued his annual selection of the best poetry printed in the nation's periodicals. Braithwaite exhibited a wide range of taste, conscientious objectivity,
and a fine capacity for exhibiting poetry that would endure. His personal
predilection for the Pre-Raphaelites and late romantics did not affect his
appreciation for other kinds of poetry. (His own verse, much overshadowed
in importance by his other writings, has a richer variety than is supposed;
though he wrote often in the manner of Ernest Dowson, his model was
sometimes Edwin Arlington Robinson, Marianne Moore, or even Dylan
Thomas.) Conservative critical pronouncements in the *Transcript* and elsewhere did nothing to enhance his influence once conservative tenets ceased
to be the rule in American poetry. And the very pursuits that brought him
prestige doomed him to a diminishing stature. No one engaged in writing
appreciative newspaper essays on poets for a livelihood could help but be

unduly generous in the long run, and no annual selection of the "best" verse, largely dependent for survival on the commercial support of poets themselves, could hold to rigid standards of excellence and a careful discrimination.

Yet poets regarded an invitation to reprint their lines in "Braithwaite" as tantamount to an award of merit; scholars still find the bibliographies and other editorial paraphernalia of these volumes valuable to their studies; and bibliophiles treasure the books because they first acclaimed poets that are now accepted as minor classics. Especially demonstrative of Braithwaite's discernment is the 1915 anthology which included E. A. Robinson's "Flammonde," Amy Lowell's "Patterns," Wallace Stevens's "Peter Quince at the Clavier," and Robert Frost's "Birches," "The Road Not Taken," and "The Death of a Hired Man." That volume also offered a poem by James Weldon Johnson, and black poets were represented in the later annuals in increasing numbers. As Margaret Haley Carpenter has said, no other annual collections of poetry "commanded the literary excitement, the prestige, or the popularity accorded these volumes." Both Braithwaite's position and disposition encouraged a wide acquaintance among aspiring and established poets; the Index of Names for correspondence in the William Stanley Braithwaite Papers at Harvard University runs to more than thirteen typed pages, single-spaced and double column. His reputation as discoverer and mentor of new talent is thoroughly deserved.

Philip Butcher, "Introduction," *The William Stanley Braithwaite Reader* (Ann Arbor: University of Michigan Press, 1972), pp. 1, 3–4

KENNY J. WILLIAMS   By 1929 Braithwaite was surveying annually over 200 magazines and newspapers. Despite the range and diversity of his sources, however, his anthologies of course only approximate inclusiveness. Still, he generally succeeds in selecting from each year's offering the best and most representative pieces. "Objective" even though personally and artistically conservative (just as ⟨Harriet⟩ Monroe was conservative), adamant that all poetic views and voices be heard, Braithwaite supported not only the Imagist movement but those younger poets who had succumbed neither to eastern traditions nor to academic conceptions of verse. Among this latter group were the bohemians and experimenters whose intensity and vitality energized American literature. Braithwaite's attentions—consistently prophetic—thrust forward avant garde writers who otherwise may have suffered neglect. ⟨. . .⟩

Monroe deals most specifically with women poets in *Poets and Their Art*; Braithwaite, however, devotes a number of years to the issue of Afro-American art, his views on it shaped and determined by his evolving aesthetic principles. Despite his apparent equivocation on racial matters, he did much to make the work of the Harlem Renaissance more accessible to the general American reading public. Yet the excesses of the movement, and especially the poetry of Claude McKay, disturbed this genteel man. Certainly, McKay's power lies partially in his own ability to embody an altered sonnet from sincere protests against an emasculating and dehumanizing system—"If We Must Die" is a case in point. But for Braithwaite the province of poetry excludes such protest, and if a lyricist recognizes McKay's innovative treatment of the sonnet tradition, as a critic he condemns him—in "The Negro in Literature," from the September 1924 issue of *The Crisis*—as a "violent and angry propagandist" who uses "his natural poetic gifts" to voice "defiant thoughts." We cannot know today the extent to which Braithwaite's antipathy was predicated on McKay's radical political associations, or his violation—in Braithwaite's view—of an "art-for-art's-sake" principle. Yet that he supported aesthetically motivated "Negro poetry" is clear; indeed, in essays appearing in such publications as *Colored American Magazine*, *The Crisis*, and *Opportunity*, Braithwaite contributes to the developing black aesthetic.

Of course, Braithwaite occasionally evinces the gentility made famous by his Boston literary circle. In his review of Jessie Fauset, for instance, he claims her novels of the middle class to be excellent studies and Fauset herself to be among the outstanding female novelists in America. In fact, he goes so far as to call her "the Jane Austen of Negro Literature."

Overt literary protest annoyed Braithwaite's sensibilities, but neither did he respect those writers who—in catering to the whimsy of white audiences—denigrate themselves. He was one of the first American critics to perceive that Paul Laurence Dunbar had ended one era of Afro-American literature and, for better or for worse, initiated another. As against Howells's claim that Dunbar represents "the soul" of his people, Braithwaite felt that he merely interprets "a folk temperament." (That neither critic pays much attention to Dunbar's standard English verse is probably not suprising.) Braithwaite rejected as well the double standard of critics and artists who insisted on the innately exotic and primitive nature of Afro-American literature. Nor could he tolerate white writers who falsified black portraits. Such racist novelists as Thomas Dixon, he argues, move "from caricature to libel"; and even the sympathetic Eugene O'Neill is unable to perceive "the immense paradox of racial life."

In an age not known for sophisticated racial advancements, Braithwaite did bridge one gap, at least, between the black and white worlds: his long association with the Boston *Evening Transcript* is ample evidence of his acceptance among the Boston Brahmins. As early as 1906, the Boston Author's Club elected him to membership, and among his close friends he counted such New Englanders as Thomas Wentworth Higginson, Julia Ward Howe, Thomas Bailey Aldrich, Bliss Perry, and Edward Everett Hale. In 1907, too, he accepted an invitation to participate in the centenary celebration of John Greenleaf Whittier's birth, for which occasion he wrote the ode "White Magic," a comparison of social and aesthetic literary modes.

⟨. . .⟩ If one can accept Braithwaite's belief that a commitment to the totality of American experience does not invalidate a specific cultural or racial heritage—if one can accept the diversity of Afro-American literature itself, and assume that *blackness* and *whiteness* need not be in themselves determining aesthetic criteria—then Braithwaite, who deserves to be remembered, ceases to be a literary phenomenon.

> Kenny J. Williams, "An Invisible Partnership and Unlikely Relationship: William Stanley Braithwaite and Harriet Monroe," *Callaloo* 10, No. 3 (Summer 1987): 548–50

Bibliography

Lyrics of Life and Love. 1904.

The Book of Elizabethan Verse (editor). 1906.

The House of Falling Leaves, with Other Poems. 1908.

The Book of Georgian Verse (editor). 1909.

The Book of Restoration Verse (editor). 1910.

Anthology of Magazine Verse for 1913 (editor). 1913.

Anthology of Magazine Verse for 1914 (editor). 1914.

Anthology for Magazine Verse for 1915 (editor). 1915.

Representative American Poetry (editor). 1916.

Anthology for Magazine Verse for 1916 and Year Book of American Poetry (editor). 1916.

The Poetic Year for 1916: A Critical Anthology (editor). 1917.

Anthology for Magazine Verse for 1917 and Year Book of American Poetry (editor). 1917.

The Golden Treasury of Magazine Verse (editor). 1918.

Anthology of Magazine Verse for 1918 and Year Book of American Poetry (editor). 1918.

Victory! Celebrated by Thirty-eight American Poets (editor). 1919.

The Story of the Great War. 1919.

Anthology of Magazine Verse for 1919 and Year Book of American Poetry (editor). 1919.

The Book of Modern British Verse (editor). 1919.

Anthology of Magazine Verse for 1920 and Year Book of American Poetry (editor). 1920.

Anthology of American Verse for 1921 and Year Book of American Poetry (editor). 1921.

Anthology of Massachusetts Poets (editor). 1922.

Anthology of Magazine Verse for 1922 and Yearbook of American Poetry (editor). 1922.

Anthology of Magazine Verse for 1923 and Yearbook of American Poetry (editor). 1923.

Anthology of Magazine Verse for 1924 and Yearbook of American Poetry (editor). 1924.

Anthology of Magazine Verse for 1925 and Yearbook of American Poetry (editor). 1925.

Anthology of Magazine Verse for 1926 and Yearbook of American Poetry (editor). 1926.

Anthology of Magazine Verse for 1927 and Yearbook of American Poetry (editor). 1927.

Anthology of Magazine Verse for 1928 and Yearbook of American Poetry (editor). 1928.

Anthology of Magazine Verse for 1929 and Yearbook of American Poetry (editor). 1929.

Our Lady's Choir: A Contemporary Anthology of Verse by Catholic Sisters (editor). 1931.

Selected Poems. 1948.

The Bewitched Parsonage: The Story of the Brontës. 1950.

The William Stanley Braithwaite Reader. Ed. Philip Butcher. 1972.

William Wells Brown

c. 1814–1884

WILLIAM WELLS BROWN was born outside Lexington, Kentucky, around 1814 to a slave named Elizabeth. He was one of seven children of Elizabeth, each of whom had a different father. It is likely that Brown's father was the half-brother of John Young, his master, although Brown was never certain of his paternity. In 1827, Brown and his family were moved to a farm north of St. Louis. Brown showed his intelligence even as a child and, instead of being sent to the fields, was hired out for work in the city. Brown's work as a printer's helper for the *St. Louis Times* and as a physician's assistant to Dr. Young provided a short reprieve from the usual trials of slavery and stimulated Brown's intellect. Later, however, Brown was hired to a slave trader, James Walker, for whom he tended slaves bound for sale in Natchez or New Orleans. This task was made no less painful for Brown when he learned that his family was being sold and separated. In 1833, after Brown failed in an escape attempt with his mother, Elizabeth, she was sold south, never to be seen again, and Brown was sold to Enoch Price.

Price proved to be Brown's last master, for on New Year's Day, 1834, Brown escaped and undertook an arduous journey to freedom. Along the road, after much hardship, Brown was taken in and nursed by a Quaker from whom he took his surname. Now free, Brown worked diligently to start a new life and in 1834 married Elizabeth Schooner, with whom he had three daughters. Brown was quickly drawn to the abolitionists and provided a link in the Underground Railroad, ferrying escaped slaves to Canada. Much affected by the speeches of Frederick Douglass, Brown also began to lecture. After unleashing his powerful and often humorous tongue, he was embraced by William Lloyd Garrison's wing of the abolitionist movement and the American Anti-Slavery Society and published many essays in abolitionist papers. Brown's lecturing schedule was relentless but he was determined to reach an even greater audience; in 1847 he published *Narrative of William W. Brown, a Fugitive Slave*, which became a best-selling antislavery work. The *Narrative* showed Brown to be highly skilled in the use of dialogue, anecdote, and argument, while powerfully retelling the dramatic scenes common to slavery and slave narratives.

In 1849 Brown, recently elected to the World Peace Congress, traveled to Europe on a lecture tour. His sojourn was turned into an exile with the passage of the Fugitive Slave Act in 1850, which prevented him from returning to the free states. Brown undertook an exhausting series of lectures in Europe for the next five years, meeting many celebrities of the day. In 1852 he published *Three Years in Europe*, a travel book; a year later appeared *Clotel; or, The President's Daughter*, the first novel to be published by a black American. This complex novel, full of plots and subplots, is a fictional account of the life of a mulatto woman rumored to be the illegitimate child of Thomas Jefferson and one of his slaves. Though the novel is occasionally fantastic in plot, Brown's use of excerpts from legal codes and religious sermons, his descriptions of slave auctions, hunts, and lynchings, and his rich portrayal of the slave mentality give it an authoritative, and sometimes epic, tone. In 1854 Brown's British friends purchased his freedom and he returned to the United States, where he published three revisions of *Clotel: Miralda; or, The Beautiful Quadroon* (serialized 1860–61); *Clotelle: A Tale of the Southern States* (1864); and *Clotelle; or, The Colored Heroine* (1867).

Brown also published a number of other works showing his versatility as a writer: *St. Domingo: Its Revolutions and Its Patriots*, a historical work; *The American Fugitive in Europe* (1855), an enlargement of his travel book; *The Escape; or, A Leap for Freedom* (1858), the first play to be published by a black American writer; a *Memoir* (1859); and *The Black Man, His Antecedents, His Genius, and His Achievements* (1863), a chronicle of the historical importance of African civilizations and contemporary black Americans.

After the Civil War Brown, like many abolitionists, continued to lecture about the plight of the newly freed slaves, as well as other issues of civil rights, such as women's suffrage. His three final books focus on the historical role of black Americans: *The Negro in the American Rebellion: His Heroism and His Fidelity* (1867); *The Rising Son* (1873); and *My Southern Home* (1880). Brown died November 6, 1884, and was buried in Cambridge, Massachusetts, in an unmarked grave.

◈ Critical Extracts

VERNON LOGGINS   It ⟨*Narrative of William W. Brown*⟩ is one of
the most readable of the slave autobiographies, mainly because it is developed
with incident rather than with comment. One story after another, such as
the following, is introduced:

> During our stay in New Orleans I met with a young white
> man with whom I was acquainted in St. Louis. He had been sold
> into slavery under the following circumstances. His father was
> a drunkard, and very poor, with a family of five or six
> children. The father died, and left the mother to take care of
> and provide for the children as best she might. The oldest
> was a boy, named Burrill, about thirteen years of age, who did
> chores in the store kept by Mr. Riley, to assist his mother
> in procuring a living for the family. After working with him for
> two years, Mr. Riley took him to New Orleans to wait on
> him while in that city on a visit, and when he returned to St.
> Louis, he told the mother of the boy that he had died with
> the yellow fever. Nothing more was heard from him, no one
> supposing him to be alive. I was much astonished when
> Burrill told me his story. Though I sympathized with him I could
> not assist him. We were both slaves. He was poor, uneducated
> and without friends; and, if living, is, I presume, still held as a
> slave.

However much the sensationalism of the book might tax the credulity of
the reader, there is interest in it. The character most completely presented,
Walker, the slave trader, far more diabolic than the terrible Covey of
Douglass' autobiographies, is perhaps as near an approach to the melodramatic villain as antislavery literature had to offer before Simon Legree
appeared in *Uncle Tom's Cabin.* The style of the *Narrative* is all the more
telling because of its simplicity. The idiom throughout is almost monosyl-
labic, such as one might expect from a runaway slave who had never been
to school. Brown drew freely from the *Narrative,* copying passages word for
word, for the autobiographical sketches with which he prefaced a number
of his later books; and it formed the basis of the *Biography of an American
Bondman,* published in 1856, the work of his daughter, Josephine Brown.

Vernon Loggins, *The Negro Author: His Development in America* (New York: Columbia
University Press, 1931), pp. 161–62

HUGH M. GLOSTER   Brown's *Clotel, or the President's Daughter: A Narrative of Slave Life in the United States* (1853), the first novel by an American Negro, was published in London and is similar to much other antislavery fiction in its depiction of the hard lot of near-whites having only a slight admixture of African blood. Capitalizing upon rumors concerning Thomas Jefferson's interracial amours and mulatto progeny, the novel presents Currer, a colored woman of Richmond, as the President's discarded mistress and the mother of his two talented children, Clotel and Althesa. The body of the narrative recounts the unhappy experiences of Currer and her daughters after the death of their benevolent owner. The most dramatic and ironical scene in the book is Clotel's escape from slave-chasers by hurling herself into the Potomac River "within plain sight of the President's house and the Capital of the Union." In American editions of the novel which appeared in 1864 and 1867—the former as *Clotelle: A Tale of the Southern States* and the latter as *Clotelle, or the Colored Heroine: A Tale of the Southern States*—there are many revisions, including the substitution of an anonymous Senator for Jefferson. The hastily moving plot of the 1867 edition begins with a sale into slavery of Agnes, a mulatto whose father was a Senator, and Isabella and Marion, her daughters by a Southern scion. Henry Linwood, a Richmond aristocrat, purchases Isabella, who subsequently becomes his mistress and the mother of his child Clotelle. Later Linwood's mother-in-law, upon discovering his extra-marital affair, separates Isabella and Clotelle and returns them to bondage. Trapped by slave hunters during an attempt to join her daughter, Isabella chooses suicide in the Potomac rather than surrender. Subsequently a French officer liberates Clotelle and carries her as his wife to India, where he is killed in military service. Afterward Clotelle marries Jerome, her slavery-time black lover whom she meets in Europe. At the outbreak of the Civil War the couple return to the United States, where Jerome meets a soldier's death in the Union Army and Clotelle acts as a nurse and secret agent. At the end of the conflict Clotelle starts a school for freedmen in Mississippi. The lives of Agnes and Marion end more tragically, the former dying in Natchez before her manumission and the latter reverting to bondage along with her two daughters after her white husband passes away. In this novel the author's primary concern is to accumulate pity-evoking hardships for his heroines, the "impassioned and voluptuous daughters of the two races,—the unlawful product of the crime of human bondage." It should be noted that Marion is perhaps the first colored character in American fiction to become the legal wife of a white citizen in this country.

Hugh M. Gloster, *Negro Voices in American Fiction* (Chapel Hill: University of North Carolina Press, 1948), pp. 25–27

BLYDEN JACKSON   The best-known summary of Negro fiction currently available is Hugh Gloster's ⟨. . .⟩ *Negro Voices in American Fiction*. It covers the field of Negro fiction from Clotel through the publication of Richard Wright's well-known *Native Son* in 1940. It contains, as one of its appendices, a bibliography of all the Negro fiction which Gloster could find for the eighty-seven years he surveys. This bibliography lists some seventy-five novels. In twenty-eight of these seventy-five prominent reference is made to one or more Negro characters who are octoroons and who struggle with problems peculiar to their octoroonness. In fourteen of the twenty-eight a girl much like Clotel, indistinguishable from white and an offspring of the Southern aristocracy, plays a leading role. Of these fourteen females only one has a black father and a white mother. In the remaining fourteen novels of the twenty-eight, nine present women who can, and, in seven of the cases, do, pass for white. That is to say, in over one-third of the Negro novels published during more than two generations the concept of the tragic mulatto is either at, or very close to, stage center in the development of the fiction. This, in spite of the obvious truth that mulattoes have never been that representative of the Negro people! Moreover, in a majority of the cases where the tragic mulatto appears, the symbol is incarnated most conspicuously in a personage much like Clotel: in a woman rather than a man; in the offspring of a white, rather than a black, father; and in a child born outside the law, but still, on the father's side at least, inside the best blood in the land. For this theme of the tragic mulatto it is far from too much to say that Clotel is a supreme embodiment of its most characteristic distinctions.

And yet, this is most curious. In the cold, clear light of reflective thought, if one were to set out deliberately to find the worst single image one could select as a master symbol for the Negro's cause in the Negro novel, remembering that that novel's major function historically has been protest, one would be hard pressed to produce a more impressive candidate for a dubious honor than Clotel. Clotel is not merely not a Negro. She is not even a good American, the one thing Negro novelists, like all serious Negro writers, have been most anxious to convince the general American public Negroes undoubtedly are. She belongs to an American *ancien régime* which never has become thoroughly naturalized on these American shores, where not the gentry and their betters, but the great, and growing, middle class has waxed strong and great, and come to represent the vested interests of a culture.

Clotel, then, for the Negro novel was a most unhappy mistake. It is gratifying, therefore, to be able to hypothecate that she also seems to be only an experiment, an experiment which Negro novelists have abandoned more and more as they have learned through trial and error the real truths of their situation.

Blyden Jackson, "A Golden Mean For The Negro Novel," *CLA Journal* 3, No. 2 (December 1959): 82–83

GERALD S. ROSSELOT   ⟨. . .⟩ the characters in *Clotel* particularly illustrate Brown's indebtedness to the romance tradition that pervaded the American novel in the nineteenth century. Since Brown's purpose is to show as many horrors of slavery as he can, hoping to bring "British influence to bear upon American slavery," he subordinates his characters, both black and white, to an eventful and sensational, rapidly moving plot wherein those horrors are detailed. Thus his characters, inadequately motivated and developed, are hurriedly and directly presented by a romancer, not a novelist. Brown offers his reader little opportunity to judge the characters or even to watch them acting out the business of their miserable lives. Rarely are they allowed to think or feel, and flattened by the author's sincere intention to persuade his audience of slavery's outrage, the characters seem a static group in which conversation is infrequent and dialogue that distinguishes and reveals character and temperament and furthers action is rarer. Brown's method is not then the indirect presentation of the novelist who shows his characters in action. Rather Brown steadily tells about his characters, what happens to them, what they mean to him. Consequently, his less than rounded characters, if they do seem real, emerge as significant symbols in the violence and anguish that slavery fostered. ⟨. . .⟩

Of the slave women Clotel is the most important character and the richest symbol. Though she shares with other black characters a common goodness and a longing for freedom, even as they nobly bear the various abuses of slavery, Clotel is still an ideal in the extreme. At the auction where she is sold for fifteen hundred dollars, she is described not only as beautiful and white, but also as a Christian, trustworthy, chaste, virtuous and moral. Later, in her alliance with Horatio Green, her white lover and owner, Clotel's genuine feeling for Green, her tender conscience and "her high poetic nature" combine with anguish and "indwelling sadness" when she considers "the unavoidable and dangerous position which the tyranny of society had awarded her . . ." and the child she has borne Green.

Clotel represents several aspects of slavery. She is Brown's first victim of sexual exploitation that accompanied the peculiar institution, and she is the victim, as a near-white slave, of cruel treatment by both whites and blacks. Brown regards her ironically as "a devoted Christian" sold "in a city thronged with churches, whose tall spires look like so many signals pointing to heaven, and whose ministers preach that slavery is a God-ordained institution!" Finally she symbolizes enduring love, courage, and heroism after she is arrested and doomed as a fugitive while attempting to find her daughter.

Ultimately Brown sees Clotel as a tragic heroine, one whose death had been determined by God to be enacted "within plain sight of the President's house and the capital of the Union. . . ." Her death is "evidence . . . of the inconquerable [sic] love of liberty the heart may inherit; as well as a fresh admonition to the slave dealer, of the cruelty and enormity of his crimes." In Clotel's "appalling tragedy" Brown senses the inevitable, ironic waste: "Such was the life and such the death of a woman whose virtues and goodness of heart would have done honour to one in a higher station of life, and who, if she had been born in any other land but that of slavery, would have been honoured and loved."

Gerald S. Rosselot, "*Clotel*, a Black Romance," *CLA Journal* 23, No. 3 (March 1980): 296–99

RICHARD O. LEWIS   Despite the obviously didactic tone and sentimental mood of Brown's fiction, the unique literary conventions of his novels do present techniques of style common to other contemporary works of his time. Brown's introduction to literature evolved first through his reading the works of classical and neoclassical writers (Homer, Virgil, Horace, Dante, Goethe, and Schiller). But Brown's melodrama, inspired by his attraction to English poetry, indicates his preference for the romanticism of Wordsworth, Shelley, Scott, and DeQuincey, whose works manifest "those [idealistic] feelings and thoughts whose very presence in peasants [e.g. slaves], children, and idiots is what proves them to be the property, not of cultivated classes alone, but of all mankind." He thus employs in conjunction with each other, many of the stylistic traits of European literary romanticism and traits of nineteenth-century American realism. ⟨. . .⟩

⟨. . .⟩ The enlightenment which Brown experienced in Europe, he especially recommended to the American public in regard to its unenlightened views about racial issues. Brown made the grand tour of Europe (1848–1854); while at Stratford-on-Avon, he had the opportunity to see "Selim, an African Prince" perform in the role of the Moor in *Othello* at the Eagle Saloon. He comments that Selim "showed that he possessed great dramatic power and skill; and his description to the senate of how he won the affections of the gentle Desdemona stamped him at once as an actor of merit." Brown found his own literary interest in Shakespeare much enriched by this personal visit to the Bard's home. ⟨. . .⟩

⟨. . .⟩ Brown experienced numerous opportunities for exposure to stage productions of Shakespearean drama performed at towns and villages along the Mississippi and Missouri Rivers, where he labored as a skilled slave for hire. He was surely familiar with Shakespeare before his European sojourn, since these plays abounded in Brown's environment, particularly along the Kentucky frontier of Brown's nativity. Over intermittently long periods, he was closely associated with work on the river, as ⟨J. Noel⟩ Heermance's biography notes: "When Brown was thirteen years old, Young [his master] moved from rural Missouri to the vicinity of St. Louis." Young subsequently hired him out to "a local innkeeper" named Freeland; "[a]fter serving with Freeland for several months, Brown was hired out as a servant on one of the steamers running between St Louis and Galena." Indeed in his own *Narrative*, Brown recalls working for William R. Culver aboard the *Missouri* and later for Capt. Otis Reynolds aboard the *Enterprise*, both Mississippi steamers. There along the Mississippi, "the plays drew picturesquely various kinds of audiences from twenty to two thousand: In rooms over billiard rooms . . . in flashy interiors . . . in the 'cities' . . . and in the villages under the Cumberland Gap" ⟨Esther C. Dunn⟩. Such research establishes that blacks were a regular part of Shakespearean drama audiences during the period of Brown's youth, as well as during the period of his later life. ⟨. . .⟩

⟨. . .⟩ Brown's protagonists parallel the heroism exhibited by white characters in the classic works of such literary masters as Shakespeare, Coleridge, Scott, and Whittier, each of whom Brown quotes when the theme or tone of their works resembles his own plot situations. Having already become familiar with traditional character types and values purveyed in Western literature, readers are constrained to accept these same values and standards when similar circumstances in literature involve Afro-American characters.

Richard O. Lewis, "Literary Conventions in the Novels of William Wells Brown," *CLA Journal* 29, No. 2 (December 1985): 130–31, 145–47, 155

BLYDEN JACKSON   ⟨. . .⟩ Brown's main function as a working abolitionist was to lecture. It has been said that in England alone, during his five years of residence there, he made a thousand speeches. "The great weakness of *Clotel*," according to Vernon Loggins, "is that enough material for a dozen novels is crowded into its two-hundred and forty-five pages." Loggins' observation may well utter its own indictment of *Clotel*. Yet it may be even more perceptive, apropos of *Clotel*, to say of it that what fills its pages is not so much a dozen novels as a dozen, or more, abolitionist lectures. For it is the art of rhetoric, rather than the disciplines of inspired narration, which seems to determine the organization and the style, in addition to the content, of *Clotel*. The novel is an abolitionist *tour de force* not only in its borrowings of subject matter. It is a succession of abolitionist diatribes in the method of its presentation. As it is episodic, it is also a progression, or really a somewhat frenzied scramble, from one *exemplum* in an abolitionist homily to another. And if Brown never creates engaging characters in *Clotel*, and never surrounds his stiffly moving marionettes there with a world that comes alive, it may easily be because he was not able to shed, even in a novel, the habits of thought and modes of literary creativity he had accustomed himself to use on an abolitionist's lecturer's platform. ⟨. . .⟩

As a work of thought (and of practical use), *Clotel* may be explored with fair rewards. The student of the Negro novel can and should, for example, conclude that Clotel herself, a stipulated quadroon, embodies the theme of the tragic mulatto, a prominent theme-to-be in the Negro novel until, and even through, the Harlem Renaissance of the 1920s. He may note that Currer, Clotel's mother, who never legally marries, is yet a matriarch, and that *Clotel*, in which men play only secondary roles, is a history of a matriarchate, except for the marriage of one of Currer's daughters to a white man in New Orleans. Thus *Clotel* may be linked, by thought, to the sociology which has expatiated at length upon matriarchy and the Negro. *Clotel* lingers in, and around, Natchez. It is there that Peck, a northerner come South, resides. Brown uses Peck to illustrate the abasement of organized religion when it capitulates to slavery. He also uses Peck the northerner to suggest the economic interest which, in northerners, could, and often did, lead them to sell their souls, in effect, to slavery. Within the penumbra of implication surrounding Peck may be readily discerned, in a reflective analysis, a train of northern shipmasters, northern millowners, northern merchants, northern bankers, and northern moneylenders. But none of the northerners in this train are really shipmasters, millowners, merchants, bankers, or moneylenders. None of them, that is, are properly imagined for a tale of fiction. All of them, if they are seen in any way, appear only because the mind, catching hold of an idea, seizes upon them as pieces that fit in to help make this idea whole. They are noumena, works of thought, and thus only of practical use. But they should be, as should be Clotel, more than that. Shadowy or not, they should approach us as through a living dream. And Clotel, of course, especially in a novel which is named after her, after a *person*, should cross that magic boundary a transcendence of which would place her beside the convincing characters of the great Victorians. That she does not, simplistic as it may be, is a measure—indeed, the measure above all other measures—of *Clotel*'s failure.

The year before the year in which *Clotel* appeared had introduced the sweeping triumph of *Uncle Tom's Cabin*. Brown knew, of course, of *Uncle Tom's Cabin*. There is no reason to doubt but that its success encouraged him. He could, in 1853, not only calculate on finding occupation for his relatively idle moments by producing *Clotel*. He could, if he was in an exhilarated mood, hitch, at least in dreams, his wagon to a best seller's star. He could, that is, daydream of writing another *Uncle Tom's Cabin*. And he could daydream, moreover, of writing it, not merely for his own financial gain, but also for the greater glory of the antislavery cause. Whatever his aspirations and motives, however, whatever his dreams and hopes—they all foundered. *Clotel* did not become another *Uncle Tom's Cabin*. Nor has Clotel ever become another Uncle Tom. She is not, and never was, a household word. Neither is the even more idealized Clotelle. Yet they are what we have, all we have, however they may be limited and bereft, of the first protagonist in a Negro novel. They establish a point of departure. And knowledge of them, whatever their condition and their goods or evils, is indispensable in a full history of the Negro novel.

    Blyden Jackson, *A History of Afro-American Literature* (Baton Rouge: Louisiana State University Press, 1989), Vol. 1, pp. 339–42

◈ *Bibliography*

Narrative of William W. Brown, a Fugitive Slave, Written by Himself. 1847, 1848.

A Lecture Delivered Before the Female Anti-Slavery Society of Salem, at Lyceum Hall, Nov. 14, 1847. 1847.

The Anti-Slavery Harp: A Collection of Songs for Anti-Slavery Meetings (editor). 1848.

A Description of William Wells Brown's Original Panoramic Views of the Scenes in the Life of an American Slave. 1849.

Three Years in Europe; or, Places I Have Seen and People I Have Met. 1852, 1855 (as *The American Fugitive in Europe: Sketches of Places and People Abroad*).

Clotel; or, The President's Daughter: A Narrative of Slave Life in the United States. 1853, 1861 (as *Miralda; or, The Beautiful Quadroon: A Romance of American Slavery, Founded on Fact*), 1864 (as *Clotelle: A Tale of the Southern States*), 1867 (as *Clotelle; or, The Colored Heroine*).

St. Domingo: Its Revolutions and Its Patriots. 1855.

The Escape; or, A Leap for Freedom. 1858.

Memoir of William Wells Brown, an American Bondman: Written by Himself. 1859.

The Black Man, His Antecedents, His Genius, and His Achievements. 1863.

The Negro in the American Rebellion: His Heroism and His Fidelity. 1867.

The Rising Son; or, The Antecedents and Advancement of the Colored Race. 1873.

My Southern Home; or, The South and Its People. 1880.

Charles W. Chesnutt
1858–1932

CHARLES WADDELL CHESNUTT was born in Cleveland, Ohio, on June 20, 1858. His parents were free blacks who moved to Fayetteville, North Carolina, after the Civil War. Chesnutt began teaching at age fourteen and from 1877 to 1880 was assistant principal of State Normal School in Fayetteville; he became principal in 1880. In 1878 he married Susan Perry, with whom he had four children. Chesnutt went to New York City in 1883 to work as a journalist; he soon relocated to Cleveland, where he studied law.

In 1887, the year he passed his bar examination, Chesnutt sold his first stories. He was "discovered" by the critic and editor Walter Hines Page, who promoted Chesnutt's work enthusiastically over the next decade. Chesnutt spent these years working as a Cleveland court reporter and writing stories. These were published in two volumes in 1899. *The Conjure Woman* contained the Uncle Julius stories, which retold tales from Ovid and Vergil in black dialect, while *The Wife of His Youth* collected a series of stories with mulatto protagonists. Encouraged by the success of these books and of his biography, *Frederick Douglass*, published the same year, Chesnutt left his job to write full-time and made a southern lecture tour. His most controversial prose works, essays concerning his hope of miscegenation in America, were published in the *Boston Transcript* in 1900. Also at this time he began exchanging letters with Booker T. Washington and was instrumental in having Macmillan withdraw from publication the antiblack volume *The American Negro*. His most popular novel was his first, *The House Behind the Cedars* (1900), which poignantly, if somewhat melodramatically, etches the difficulties of mixed-race offspring in the South.

The Marrow of Tradition (1901) was a sweeping condemnation of racial prejudice and greed, less sentimental than its predecessor and correspondingly less popular. Chesnutt was disappointed by the book's failure, and in 1902 he returned to his court reporting position. He wrote another novel, *The Colonel's Dream* (1905), as well as at least five more that remain unpublished. An outspoken advocate for black rights, he successfully shut down the showing of *The Birth of a Nation* in Ohio, often protested the treatment of black soldiers, and was honored with the NAACP's Spingarn Medal in 1928. After years of strokes and ill health Charles Chesnutt died at his home in Cleveland on November 15, 1932. His daughter Helen published a memoir of him in 1952.

◈ *Critical Extracts*

WILLIAM DEAN HOWELLS   The critical reader of the story called "The Wife of His Youth," which appeared in these pages two years ago, must have noticed uncommmon traits in what was altogether a remarkable piece of work. The first was the novelty of the material, for the writer dealt not only with people who were not white, but with people who were not black enough to contrast with white people—who were in fact of that near approach to the ordinary American in race and color which leaves, at the last degree, every one but the connoisseur in doubt whether they are Anglo-Saxon or Anglo-African. Quite as striking as this novelty of the material was the author's thorough mastery of it, and his unerring knowledge of the life he had chosen in its peculiar racial characteristics. But above all, the story was notable for the passionless handling of a phase of our common life which is tense with potential tragedy; for the attitude, almost ironical, in which the artist observes the play of contesting emotions in the drama under his eyes; and for his apparently reluctant, apparently helpless consent to let the spectator know his real feeling in the matter. Anyone accustomed to study methods in fiction, to distinguish between good and bad art, to feel the joy which the delicate skill possible only from a love of truth can give, must have known a high pleasure in the quiet self-restraint of the performance; and such a reader would probably have decided that the social situation in the piece was studied wholly from the outside, by an observer with special opportunities for knowing it, who was, as it were, surprised into final sympathy.

Now, however, it is known that the author of this story is of negro blood—diluted, indeed, in such measure that if he did not admit this descent few would imagine it, but still quite of that middle world which lies next, though wholly outside, our own. Since his first story appeared he has contributed several others to these pages, and he now makes a showing palpable to criticism in a volume called *The Wife of His Youth, and Other Stories of the Color Line* ⟨. . .⟩

William Dean Howells, "Mr. Charles W. Chesnutt's Stories," *Atlantic Monthly* 85, No. 5 (May 1900): 699–701

CHARLES W. CHESNUTT   The popular theory is that the future American race will consist of the harmonious fusion of the various European elements which now make up our heterogeneous population. The result is to be something infinitely superior to the best of the component elements. This perfection of type—for no good American could for a moment doubt that it will be as perfect as everything else American—is to be brought about by a combination of all the best characteristics of the different European races, and the elimination, by some strange alchemy, of all their undesirable traits—for even a good American will admit that European races, now and then, have some undesirable traits when they first come over. It is a beautiful, a hopeful, and to the eye of faith, a thrilling prospect. ⟨. . .⟩

By the eleventh census ⟨1890⟩, the ratios of which will probably not be changed materially by the census now under way, the total population of the United States was about 65,000,000, of which about seven million were black and colored, and something over 200,000 were of Indian blood. It is then in the three broad types—white, black and Indian—that the future American race will find the material for its formation. Any dream of a pure white race, of the Anglo-Saxon type, for the United States, may as well be abandoned as impossible, even if desirable. That such future race will be predominantly white may well be granted—unless the climate in the course of time should modify existing types; that it will call itself white is reasonably sure; that it will conform closely to the white type is likely; but that it will have absorbed and assimilated the blood of the other two races mentioned is as certain as the operation of any law well can be that deals with so uncertain a quantity as the human race.

There are no natural obstacles to such an amalgamation. The unity of the race is not only conceded but demonstrated by actual crossing. Any theory of sterility due to race crossing may as well be abandoned; it is founded mainly on prejudice and cannot be proved by the facts. If it come from Northern or European sources, it is likely to be weakened by lack of knowledge; if from Southern sources it is sure to be colored by prejudice. My own observation is that in a majority of cases people of mixed blood are very prolific and very long-lived. The admixture of races in the United

States has never taken place under conditions likely to produce the best results; but there have nevertheless been enough conspicuous instances to the contrary in this country, to say nothing of a long and honorable list in other lands, to disprove the theory that people of mixed blood, other things being equal, are less virile, prolific or able than those of purer strains. But whether this be true or not is apart from this argument. Admitting that races may mix, and that they are thrown together under conditions which permit their admixture, the controlling motive will be not abstract considerations with regard to a remote posterity, but present interest and inclination.

Charles W. Chesnutt, "The Future American" (1900), MELUS 15, No. 3 (Fall 1988): 96–98

WILLIAM STANLEY BRAITHWAITE   The development of fiction among Negro authors has been, I might almost say, one of the repressed activities of our literary life. A fair start was made the last decade of the nineteenth century when Chestnutt and Dunbar were turning out both short stories and novels. In Dunbar's case, had he lived, I think his literary growth would have been in the evolution of the Race novel as indicated in The Uncalled and Sport of the Gods. ⟨. . .⟩ His contemporary, Charles W. Chestnutt, was concerned more primarily with the fiction of the Color Line and the contacts and conflicts of its two worlds. He was in a way more successful. In the five volumes to his credit, he has revealed himself as a fiction writer of a very high order. But after all Mr. Chestnutt is a story-teller of genius transformed by racial earnestness into the novelist of talent. His natural gift would have found freer vent in a flow of short stories like Bret Harte's, to judge from the facility and power of his two volumes of short stories, The Wife of His Youth and Other Stories and The Conjure Woman. But Mr. Chestnutt's serious effort was in the field of the novel, where he made a brave and partially successful effort to correct the distortions of Reconstruction fiction and offset the school of Page and Cable. Two of these novels, The Marrow of Tradition and The House Behind the Cedars, must be reckoned among the representative period novels of their time. But the situation was not ripe for the great Negro novelist. The American public preferred spurious values to the genuine; the coinage of the Confederacy was at literary par. Where Dunbar, the sentimentalist, was welcome, Chestnutt, the realist, was barred. In 1905 Mr. Chestnutt wrote The Colonel's Dream, and thereafter silence fell upon him.

William Stanley Braithwaite, "The Negro in American Literature," The New Negro: An Interpretation, ed. Alain Locke (New York: Albert & Charles Boni, 1925), pp. 42–43

HELEN M. CHESNUTT   Chesnutt's love of life was so great, his interest in the world and its problems so vital that he seemed to those who loved him perennially young. His gallant humor, his love for people, his keen enjoyment of all the little things in life never grew less. A passion for human justice possessed him; for justice he worked throughout his life.

His conception of human rights was simple. Rights are fundamental. Man does not have to earn them; does not have to struggle to be worthy of gaining them at some far-off future time. Rights are given by God and are inalienable, and any human being that does not demand his rights, all of them, is lacking in integrity and is something less than a man.

His philosophy for himself and his family was characteristic:

"We are normal human beings with all the natural desires of normal individuals. We acknowledge no inherent inferiority and resent any denial of rights and opportunities based on racial discrimination. We believe in equality and all that it implies. We shall live our lives as Americans pure and simple, and whatever experiences we encounter shall be borne with forbearance, and fortitude, and amusement if possible."

His children were nurtured on this philosophy which became a part of their mental and spiritual inheritance.

Chesnutt enjoyed a rich, full life. Starting out at the age of fourteen to earn his living, he had been able by his own efforts, with the assistance of what tutors he could find, to acquire a fine liberal education. He was an ardent reader and loved all kinds of books. In his later years the books on his bedside table showed his wide range of interest. *The Odes of Horace*, the latest French book, a mystery story, a current best-seller; the *Story of Philosophy*, the *Atlantic*, the *Crisis*, *Opportunity*, the *Nation*, the *New Republic*—all gave him interest and pleasure. He loved music and the theatre and, until his health became too poor, attended with his wife and daughters the many concerts and plays that have enriched the lives of Clevelanders. He loved beauty and was able to store his mind with the beauties of nature by extensive travel in America and parts of Europe.

But he was human and had his weaknesses. He was not a good business man. His real-estate ventures were always a hazard because of his forbearance—some of his tenants exploited him outrageously. He, like many others, suffered serious financial losses in the crash of the stock market in 1929. But he never grew cynical. Life to him was a beautiful thing.

He experienced in abundance the things that make life beautiful—aspiration, high endeavor, noted achievement, and widespread recognition; then disillusion, readjustment, service to mankind, the respect and affection of all who knew him, abiding love and devotion from every member of his family.

Helen M. Chesnutt, *Charles Waddell Chesnutt: Pioneer of the Color Line* (Chapel Hill: University of North Carolina Press, 1952), pp. 311–12

NIKKI GIOVANNI   *The Conjure Woman* puts Joel Chandler Harris and Stephen Foster and all those dudes up to and including ⟨William⟩ Styron in their places. Uncle Julius is out to win. And he does. He convinces the cracker that the grapes have a spell on them and are therefore better left alone. He shows what would happen if the white man had to live in the Black man's shoes in "Mars Jeems's Nightmare." And he keeps his nephew's job for him. He uses the white woman's natural curiosity about Black men to his advantage. She always sympathizes with him while her husband is prone to back off. He is a good Black politician. The cracker gives the lumber that is "Po'Sandy" to the Black church. Uncle Julius is one of Black literature's most exciting characters precisely because he is so definite about his aims. He intends to see his people come out on top. John, the white voice, thought he could use Julius while it was the other way around. And Chesnutt drops a few gems on us dispelling the romantic theory about slavery's charms.

Nikki Giovanni, *Gemini: An Extended Autobiographical Statement on My First Twenty-five Years of Being a Black Poet* (Indianapolis: Bobbs-Merrill, 1971), pp. 100–101

WILLIAM L. ANDREWS   One reason why "Baxter's Procrustes" epitomizes Chesnutt's work in the short story is that it revives and refines some of the most distinctive satiric techniques of his conjure and color line stories. Describing Chesnutt's last *Atlantic* story as one in which a hoax is perpetrated on a group of self-assured but self-deluded gentlemen helps to place "Baxter's Procrustes" in a tradition which embraces such works as "The Conjurer's Revenge," "A Matter of Principle," and "The Passing of Grandison." In each of these earlier stories an ostensibly innocuous but unexpectedly cunning subordinate—a handyman, an office assistant, and a slave—exposes the prejudices of his patron and supposed superior, by playing false roles and manipulating illusory situations so as to capitalize upon his superior's inability to look below the surface of things. The trickster triumphs simply by allowing the deceived to deceive themselves. Thus at the end of such diverse stories as "Baxter's Procrustes," "A Matter of Principle," or "The Passing of Grandison," the reader learns a good deal about deception though (and probably because) the duped does not. Similar to its predecessors, "Baxter's Procrustes" uses an irony mixed with pathos to elicit from the reader an Horatian smile of amusement at the follies of men. The reader is encouraged to laugh, but not too loudly or too long, for, like Chesnutt, his feeling of superiority to the Bodleians' investment-consciousness or the Blue Veins' social exclusivism will be tempered by a poignant recognition of his own sympathies with the now-questionable "principles" of these "best people" of American and Afro-American society.

What marks "Baxter's Procrustes" as an advancement over its forebears in Chesnutt's fiction is its attention to the character of the confidence man himself. Usually hardly more than a device or an authorial mouthpiece, the hoaxer in "Baxter's Procrustes" is characterized in almost as much detail as the hoaxed. Chesnutt seems at pains to individualize his hoaxer, even to the point of hinting at his past, his personal circumstances, his motives, and his "philosophy" of life. Apparently Chesnutt wanted his reader to pay as much attention to the hoaxer as to the effect of his hoax. The reason for this attempt to establish a bond of sympathy between Baxter and the reader becomes clearer as one examines the character of Baxter. For this is no ordinary hoaxer, not merely an instrument by which Chesnutt took his mocking revenge on the delusions of the socially pretentious and the racially "superior." Baxter is Chesnutt's most elaborate self-dramatization, the most transparent and close-fitting of the many masks the author assumed in his fiction. Baxter's satirical purpose derives from Chesnutt's apparent presentation of his own artistic situation in 1904 through that of Baxter, an unsuccessful author who is patronized, summarized, and categorized by an ignorant, commercially minded, pseudo-literary readership.

William L. Andrews, *The Literary Career of Charles W. Chesnutt* (Baton Rouge: Louisiana State University Press, 1980), pp. 213–14

DONALD B. GIBSON   In his diary of July 31, 1875, Chesnutt made the following observation:

> Twice today, or oftener, I have been taken for "white." At the pond this morning one fellow said he'd "be damned if there was any nigger blood in me." At Coleman's I passed. On the road an old chap, seeing the trunks, took me for a student coming from school. I believe I'll leave here and pass anyhow, for I am as white as any of them. One old fellow said today, "Look here, Tom. Here's a black as white as you are."

Chesnutt expresses a paradox here, a paradox touching upon the essence of his self-conception. He indicates the disparity between illusion and reality, perception and knowledge. He deals with the enigma of the thing that is what it is not, and is not what it is: "Here's a black as white as you are." His "I am as white as any of them" is only meaningful in context coming from a person who does not conceive of himself as white. Although Chesnutt indicates the attitude that it is better to be white than black, his own personal decision when he confronted the possibility of passing was not to pass. His decision was not so much to be black as not to have distinguished between himself as mulatto and individuals more purely Negro. Speaking at the time of his reception of the NAACP's Spingarn Medal in 1928, Chesnutt says,

> ... substantially all of my writings, with the exception of *The Conjure Woman*, have dealt with the problems of people of mixed blood, which, while in the main the same as those of the true Negro, are in some instances and in some respects more complex and difficult of treatment, in fiction as in life.

He sometimes refers indirectly to himself as "Negro" or "colored" but never directly. At one time he refers to himself as "an American of acknowledged African descent," but he follows that with, "In this case the infusion of African blood is very small—is not in fact a visible admixture."

At work in Chesnutt's paradoxical, multifaceted attitudes about his racial identity (and about his identity generally since race is an integral part of identity) is a particular habit of mind that allowed (or perhaps caused?) him to hold contradictory ideas at the same moment. It is what I would call the dialectical habit of mind, a way of perceiving the world in terms of ideas standing in opposing relation. In Chesnutt's case, opposing ideas may stand in diametrical opposition, but the opposing elements are not of equal weight; hence an idea or belief that Chesnutt strongly holds will be pitted against a contradictory idea, also within his scheme of values, of lesser weight or strength. Concretely expressed, Dr. Miller in *The Marrow of Tradition* embodies a great number of Chesnutt's own values, beliefs, and feelings, but Chesnutt's doubt about the validity of those values, beliefs, and feelings finds an objectification in the character of Josh Green. The two characters exist in thesis-antithesis relation.

Again to express concretely the dialectical character of his thought, we may take Chesnutt's expression of optimism and pessimism as an example. On the one hand, Chesnutt's characters (and the man himself as the diary indicates) are usually optimistic and hopeful of the accomplishment of some desired end. On the other, they are thwarted so frequently and so completely as to suggest the impossibility of achieving anything resembling human happiness. A third turn of the screw suggests that some force, some agency outside human experience, in some measure rights things. Hence murderers are usually punished; evil is frequently revenged as the imbalance caused by the commission of wrong-doing is frequently restored, betokening an ordered world. These attitudes, the optimistic and the pessimistic, find expression within the same contexts. At the end of his darkest tale, "The Web of Circumstance," Chesnutt attempts to relieve the gloom by appending a paragraph in which he, as author, speaks:

> Some time, we are told, when the cycle of years has rolled around,
> there is to be another golden age, when all men will dwell
> together in love and harmony, and when peace and righteousness
> shall prevail for a thousand years. God speed the day and
> ... give us here and there, and now and then, some little foretaste
> of this golden age, that we may the more patiently and hopefully
> await its coming!

This paragraph was necessary in order to counteract the meaning of the tale itself. Although inclined to believe that life as lived is essentially tragic, Chesnutt never intends to go so far as to suggest that life (and ultimately history) is without meaning, as the tale indeed suggests. No "foretaste of a golden age" is visible there; so Chesnutt, in the final passage of the tale and of the book, makes a statement entirely contrary to the meaning of this particular tale, as well as to the implications of some of the others. Once again in his fiction, antithesis undercuts and hence qualifies thesis.

The tension resulting from opposing elements forms the center of nearly all his fiction. Irony, paradox (of character and situation, not language and style), and ambivalence are his stock in trade. In his most complex work, theses, countertheses, subtheses, and countersubtheses play off against one another, revealing a subtlety of mind easily obscured by his formal style, diction, and traditional technique. This subtle play of mind, the awareness and expression of myriad gradations of thought and feeling, is another element distinguishing Chesnutt from the majority of his contemporaries.

Donald B. Gibson, "Charles W. Chesnutt: The Anatomy of a Dream," *The Politics of Literary Expression: A Study of Major Black Writers* (Westport, CT: Greenwood Press), 1981, pp. 125–28

SALLYANN H. FERGUSON   Scholarship on novelist and short story writer Charles W. Chesnutt stagnates in recent years because his critics have failed to address substantively the controversial issues raised by his essays. Indeed, many scholars either minimize or ignore the fact that these writings complement his fiction and, more importantly, that they often reveal unflattering aspects of Chesnutt the social reformer and artist. In a much-quoted journal entry of 16 March 1880, Chesnutt himself explicitly links his literary art with social reform, saying he would write for a "high, holy purpose," "not so much [for] the elevation of the colored people as the elevation of the whites." Using the most sophisticated artistic skills at his command, he ultimately hopes to expose the latter to a variety of positive and non-stereotypic images of the "colored people" and thereby mitigate white racism. As he remarks in a 29 May 1880 entry, "it is the province of literature to open the way for him [the colored person] to get it [equality]— to accustom the public mind to the idea; and while amusing them [whites], to lead people out, imperceptibly, unconsciously, step by step, to the desired state of feeling." Throughout his entire literary career, Chesnutt never strays far from these basic reasons for writing, in fiction and nonfiction alike.

It is in his essays, however, that Chesnutt most clearly reveals the limited nature of his social and literary goals. Armed with such familiar journal passages as those cited above, scholars have incorrectly presumed that this writer seeks to use literature primarily as a means for alleviating white color prejudice against *all* black people in this country. But, while the critics romantically hail him as a black artist championing the cause of his people, Chesnutt, as his essays show, is essentially a social and literary accommodationist who pointedly and repeatedly confines his reformist impulses to the "colored people"—a term that he almost always applies either to color-line blacks or those of mixed races. This self-imposed limitation probably stems from the fact that he wrote during a time of intense color hatred in America, when the masses of blacks, because of their dark skin, could not unobtrusively be assimilated into the mainstream culture. Chesnutt was well aware that the dismal plight of these "genuine negro[es]" (as he calls dark-skinned blacks in a 30 May 1889 *New York Independent* essay entitled "What Is a White Man?") was not amenable to his kind of artistic stealth and subtlety and required more aggression. In his "White Man" essay, therefore, the pacifist author stresses the futility of such a measure, arguing that force can have little effect in bringing about equal citizenship for black people of any hue. After discarding both force and non-violence as potential remedies for the predicament of "genuine Negroes" in America, Chesnutt must have viewed their plight as virtually insoluble. Thus, it is not surprising that the author deliberately limits his goals to that which he believed he could reasonably accomplish—to improving the lot of the "colored people," as he indicates very early in his career. ⟨. . .⟩

The "Future American" series and other essays by Chesnutt reveal how his self-imposed social and literary mission is essentially at odds with racial realities, a dilemma that accounts for his often contradictory views. For instance, in the "White Man" article discussed earlier, he is forced to criticize Southern whites for failing to enforce conflicting miscegenation laws, which he despises, in order to protect the rights of the "colored people" these laws might benefit. Perhaps his daughter Helen, who subtitled the first biography of her father, *Pioneer of the Color Line* (1952), understood best the purpose of her father's life and work. Present-day scholars may attain similar understanding if we begin to re-examine Chesnutt's fiction in light of his nonfiction. It may be that after blackness came into vogue, we grew too content with merely celebrating black literary achievement. Nonetheless, before African-American literature gains a solid footing in academe, it must undergo the same kind of tough critical scrutiny to which other literatures have been subjected. Although disputed by others, Chesnutt's published essays indicate that he was among the first "African-American" literary artists to break ranks with the race and openly advocate miscegenation. In his quest to bring racial peace and a taste of the good life to the light-skinned segment of the black population, he did not hesitate to sacrifice the interests of dark-skinned people. In this latter respect, Charles W. Chesnutt is oddly callous for an otherwise sensitive man—and, ironically enough, not very different from the white founding fathers of America.

SallyAnn H. Ferguson, "Chesnutt's Genuine Blacks and Future Americans," *MELUS* 15, No. 3 (Fall 1988): 109–10, 117–18

HENRY LOUIS GATES, JR.　　　Between 1899, when he published *The Conjure Woman*, a collection of short stories, and 1905 Chesnutt published six books, including five works of fiction and a short biography of Frederick Douglass. Of these, the work that for many scholars stands as his greatest achievement is his novel *The Marrow of Tradition*. Based upon the 1989 race riot at Wilmington, North Carolina, which Chesnutt researched for two years, *The Marrow of Tradition* is one of the earliest explorations of literary naturalism in the black tradition. Here, character and fate are determined by heredity and custom. Post-Reconstruction southern social conventions, customs, and mores, Chesnutt shows us, were not as they had been represented in the neoplantation fictions so popular in the last two decades of the nineteenth century, which sought to rewrite the history of slavery with nostalgia and romanticism, through a hazy filter of "moonbeams and magnolia blossoms." No, the South that emerged after Reconstruction was just as corrupt, dishonest, and racist as southern society had been before the war. While the forms of a supposedly "new" South might differ in outward appearance from the old, in substance the two were fundamentally the same.

Indeed, the book is profoundly pessimistic ⟨. . .⟩ And yet Chesnutt's narrative skill enables him to limn this world with nuance and intelligence.

Henry Louis Gates, Jr., "Introduction," *Three Classic African American Novels* (New York: Vintage Classics, 1990), pp. xv–xvi

---

ERIC SELINGER   Charles Chesnutt claimed the order of stories in *The Conjure Woman* was "not essential." The volume has another tale to tell. While indeed "not, strictly, a novel," the collection unfolds by an ominous logic: a sequence of stories, a series of frames, through which we can see Chesnutt confronting, subverting, but ultimately underwriting certain powerful images, not just of slavery or of African-Americans, in general, but of that figure peculiarly threatening to whites of the post-Reconstruction era, the black man. Readers have, of course, noted the gender division of the work's inscribed audience, the skeptical transplanted Ohian John and his sickly, sympathetic wife Annie—indeed, John himself comments upon it several times within the text. But sexual dynamics are central to the stories Julius tells as well, in his representation of black families and romances disrupted or destroyed by slavery, and in his remarkably contrasting portrayals of conjure women (Aunt Peggy and Tenie) and equally powerful, but more dangerous conjure men. An exploration of the threefold sexual politics of the book—in Julius's stories, in the world of their telling, and the crossroads of frame and tale—reveals the coherence of the *The Conjure Woman*, a strategic structure of overplot to the book as a whole. Increasingly capable, signifying and significant through the first five stories, manipulating John's and or Annie's generic expectations—what such a storyteller will talk to them about, and how he will do so—, Julius is symbolically castrated at the end of "The Gray Wolf's Ha'nt." And in "Hot-Foot Hannibal," the closing piece, after enabling the reconciliation of North and South in the persons of Annie's younger sister Mabel and the local gentleman Malcolm Murchison, he softly and silently vanishes.

That the collection's structure should involve issues of genre as much as gender issues should come as no surprise. As Richard Yarborough has argued, "much of the fiction produced by Afro-Americans before World War I" displays "not a desire to render black life as accurately and honestly as possible," but a similar manipulation of reader response: "a willingness to dissemble, to overemphasize, even to misrepresent—that is, to write with the aim of soliciting sympathy from the white reader." But the price of such sympathy, at least for male characters, involves a sacrifice of certain "manly" virtues, most notably the willingness to use violence in self-defense, in favor of those "feminine" values of self-sacrifice, nonviolence, and family preservation which undergird the sentimental novel in general, and the troublesome but influential model of Stowe's *Uncle Tom's Cabin* in particular. ". . . rage, bitterness, and a desire for revenge on the part of positively portrayed black figures," Yarborough explains, "must be curbed in order to establish them as self-controlled, all-forgiving, and eminently acceptable candidates for membership in the American mainstream." This is doubly true when these figures are male. Such restraint risks relying on "the antebellum stereotype of blacks as loyal, faithful retainers," never agitated except when provoked by outsiders; but any hint to the contrary risks invoking in white readers' minds the notion of African-American "savagery," with its implications of riot and rape, that lynch mobs claimed to be on guard against.

As Chesnutt demonstrates in Julius's shifting narrative fortunes, the more a tale departs from sentimental norms, the less interest it provokes in, and the less power it has over, its intended white audience. (The one apparent exception, "The Conjuror's Revenge," when read in context, proves the rule.) If, as Richard Baldwin contends, Chesnutt set himself the task in this volume of changing white perceptions of blacks, and not simply of touching white sentiments, we must admit that by the end of the collection this project has been abandoned as a failure. While Uncle Julius is not exactly the sort of black male heroine available since Stowe as a white-acceptable stereotype—his association with conjure, and not Christianity, complicates the issue—, the collection closes with a decisive move toward sentimentality in the plantation-story idiom that defuses the racial and sexual issues that seem to be building toward an explosion in certain earlier tales. The otherwise troubling, unimpressive end to the collection can be read, not as an artistic lapse, but as a strategic comment on the limits authors like Chesnutt worked within and against—including, perhaps, the definitions of masculinity and femininity his conjure figures suggest.

Eric Selinger, "Aunts, Uncles, Audience: Gender and Genre in Charles Chesnutt's *The Conjure Woman*," *Black American Literature Forum* 25, No. 4 (Winter 1991): 665–67

❖ Bibliography

Frederick Douglass. 1899.

The Wife of His Youth and Other Stories of the Color Line. 1899.

The Conjure Woman. 1899.

The House Behind the Cedars. 1900.

The Marrow of Tradition. 1901.

The Colonel's Dream. 1905.

Short Fiction. Ed. Sylvia Lyons Render. 1974.

Martin R. Delany
1812–1885

MARTIN ROBISON DELANY was born free on May 6, 1812, in Charles Town, Virginia (now West Virginia), the son of Samuel and Pati Delany. Although a state law prohibited the education of black children, Delany and his siblings received informal schooling from a white man; when it was discovered that they were literate, the family was forced to flee to Chambersburg, Pennsylvania. In 1831 Delany went to Pittsburgh, where he continued his education with the Reverend Lewis Woodson and studied medicine with Dr. Andrew N. McDowell. He became politically active, joining the Abstinence Society and becoming executive secretary of the Philanthropic Society, which helped free blacks to settle in the North.

In 1843 Delany married Catherine A. Richards, with whom he had thirteen children, although four died in infancy. In 1847 he began editing the *Mystery*, one of the earliest black newspapers; later that year, however, he was forced to give up the editorship of the paper for financial reasons. He then joined with Frederick Douglass in editing the *North Star*, but his increasingly radical views on the place of blacks in American society led to a split with Douglass in 1849. In 1850 he attempted to pursue his medical studies, enrolling in the Harvard Medical School along with two other black students; but their mere presence was so disruptive that they were not allowed to return for a second term.

In the 1850s Delany began openly espousing black emigration to Africa. In his first polemical work, *The Condition, Elevation, Emigration, and Destiny of the Colored People of the United States*, which he published at his own expense in 1852, he recommended an emigration of blacks to Central America. In 1854 he called a National Emigration Convention in Cleveland, at which he delivered a fiery speech, "Political Destiny of the Colored Race on the American Continent."

In 1856 Delany, evidently disgusted with the increasing oppression of blacks in the United States, moved to Chatham, Canada, where he practiced medicine. Here he continued work on his only novel, *Blake; or, The Huts of America*, begun in 1852 and possibly inspired in part by a trip to the South he had taken in 1839. It appeared in an incomplete serialization in the *Anglo-African* for January–July 1859, and in complete form in the *Weekly Anglo-African* from November 23, 1861, to April 1862; it did not appear as a book until 1970. *Blake* is the story of Henricus Blacus, a slave who flees his master in Louisiana and migrates to Canada. Traveling to Cuba, Blake leads a force of black insurrectionists intent on preventing the annexation of Cuba by the United States. The militancy of *Blake* was almost unheard of in its day, and it would be almost a century before the novel received recognition as a pioneering work of black American fiction.

Between 1859 and 1861 Delany traveled to the Niger Valley in the hope of establishing a colony there for black Americans; he wrote of his voyage in *Official Report of the Niger Valley Exploring Party* (1861). But the plan for emigration came to nothing. In 1863 Delany began recruiting black soldiers to fight against the South in the Civil War, and in February 1865 he was appointed the first black major in the U.S. army. He pursued his recruiting activities in South Carolina, and also joined the Freedman's Bureau. He remained in South Carolina after the war, unsuccessfully running for lieutenant governor in 1874.

In his later years Delany continued lecturing on the notion of Pan-Africanism. His final work, *Principia of Ethnology* (1879), advocates the superiority of pure-blooded Africans over mulattoes, asserting that the early Ethiopian and Egyptian cultures are the source of many important developments in language, politics, and religion. Delany spent his final years with his family in Xenia, Ohio, where he died on January 24, 1885.

Delany's work was ignored for decades after his death, but in the 1920s a revival slowly began, as black critics took note of his pioneering views on Pan-Africanism, views that were propounded years before the birth of Marcus Garvey. Delany's place as a leading black American writer of the nineteenth century is now secure.

▨ *Critical Extracts*

WILLIAM WELLS BROWN   Dr. Delany has long been before the public. His first appearance, we believe, was in connection with *The Mystery*, a weekly newspaper published at Pittsburgh, and of which he was editor. His journal was faithful in its advocacy of the rights of man, and had the reputation of being a well-conducted sheet. The doctor afterwards was associated with Frederick Douglass in the editorial management of his paper at Rochester, N.Y. From the latter place he removed to Canada, and has since resided in Chatham, where he is looked upon as one of its leading citizens.

Dr. M. R. Delany, though regarded as a man high in his profession, is better and more widely known as a traveller, discoverer, and lecturer. His association with Professor Campbell in the "Niger Valley Exploring Expedition" has brought the doctor very prominently before the world, and especially that portion of it which takes an interest in the civilization of Africa. The official report of that expedition shows that he did not visit that country with his eyes shut. His observations and suggestions about the climate, soil, diseases, and natural productions of Africa, are interesting, and give evidence that the doctor was in earnest. The published report, of which he is the author, will repay a perusal.

On his return home, Dr. Delany spent some time in England, and lectured in the British metropolis and the provincial cities, with considerable success, on Africa and its resources. As a member of the International Statistical Congress, he acquitted himself with credit to his position and honor to his race. The foolish manner in which the Hon. Dr. Dallas, our minister to the court of St. James, acted on meeting Dr. Delany in that august assembly, and the criticisms of the press of Europe and America, will not soon be forgotten.

He is short, compactly built, has a quick, wiry walk, and is decided and energetic in conversation, unadulterated in race, and proud of his complexion. Though somewhat violent in his gestures, and playing but little regard to the strict rules of oratory, Dr. Delany is, nevertheless, an interesting, eloquent speaker. Devotedly attached to his fatherland, he goes for a "Negro Nationality." Whatever he undertakes, he executes it with all the powers that God has given him; and what would appear as an obstacle in the way of other men, would be brushed aside by Martin R. Delany.

William Wells Brown, *The Black Man, His Antecedents, His Genius, and His Achievements* (New York: Thomas Hamilton, 1863), pp. 174–75

ABRAHAM LINCOLN   Do not fail to have an interview with this most extraordinary and intelligent black man.

Abraham Lincoln, Letter to Edwin M. Stanton (8 February 1865), *The Collected Works of Abraham Lincoln*, ed. Roy B. Basler (New Brunswick, NJ: Rutgers University Press, 1953), Vol. 8, p. 272

FRANK A. ROLLIN   Illustrating in his career entire personal sacrifice for the accomplishment of a grand purpose, no character has been
produced by our civilization in comparison with which this remarkable man
would be deemed inferior. Men have died for the freedom and elevation of
the race, and thereby have contributed more to advance the cause than
would their living efforts, while others have lived for it, and under circumstances where death would have been easier. Such describes Martin Delany.
Nature marked him for combat and victory, and not for martyrdom. His
life-long service, from which neither poverty nor dangers could deter him,
his great vitality and energy under all and every circumstance, which have
never abated, proclaim this truth. His life furnishes a rare enthusiasm for
race not expected in the present state of American society, occasioned by
his constant researches into anything relative to their history. No living
man is better able to write the history of the race, to whom it has been a
constant study, than he; as it is considered by the most earnest laborers in
the same sphere that few, if any, among them, have so entirely consecrated
themselves to the idea of race as his career shows. His religion, his writings,
every step in life, is based upon this idea. His creed begins and ends with
it—that the colored race can only obtain their true status as men, by relying
on their own identity; that they must prove, by merit, all that white men
claim; then color would cease to be an objection to their progress—that
the blacks must take pride in being black, and show their claims to superior
qualities, before the whites would be willing to concede them equality. This
he claims as the foundation of his manhood. Upon this point Mr. Frederick
Douglass once wittily remarked, "Delany stands so straight that he leans a
little backward."

Such is the personal history of an individual of the race, whose great
strength of character, amid the multitudinous agencies adverse to his progress, has triumphantly demonstrated negro capability for greatness in every
sphere wherein he has acted.

    Frank A. Rollin, *Life and Public Services of Martin R. Delany* (Boston: Lee & Shepard,
    1868), pp. 299–301.

FREDERICK DOUGLASS   Your well known zeal and ability, and
your long devotion to the cause of freedom and equality to all men, will,
I am sure, obtain for the elaborate letter with which you have honored me,
through the columns of the Charleston *Daily Republican*, and which is now
printed in the columns of the *New National Era*, a thoughtful perusal by
intelligent colored men in all parts of this country. While I heartily concur

in much that you say in that letter, there are some things in it from which
I as heartily dissent. It is, however, due to say that, even where I dissent
from your views, I am compelled to respect your boldness, candor, and manly
independence in the utterance of your convictions. Especially and sincerely
do I thank you for your masterly exposure of the malign influences which
surrounded the whole business of reconstruction in South Carolina and the
other seceding States. I have, however, no tears to shed over that part of
our past, and no denunciations for the carpetbaggers who assumed the
leadership in the matter of reconstruction. Upon the whole, they have done
pretty well—at any rate, their prominence was inevitable, and I am disposed
to make the best of it. Your narrative is strong and striking, but not strange.
The destitution of political knowledge among the newly enfranchised and
emancipated people of South Carolina, the sullen contempt and indifference
with which the old slave-holding class looked upon all efforts to bring that
State into harmonious relations to the National Government, the absence
of any middle class among the native white population, possessed of sufficient
intelligence and patriotism to take the lead in the needed work of reorganiza-
tion, the pressing necessity for the early consummation of that work, not
only reconcile me to the employment of such hands as were found ready
to engage in that work, but to make me thankful that any were found to
lead in its performance. ⟨. . .⟩

I cannot agree with you in denouncing colored men for going armed to
political meetings in South Carolina, nor can I agree with you that the
practice is an imported one. The habit of carrying deadly weapons in the
South belongs to an age considerably earlier than that of the carpetbaggers.
I may be wrong, but I had supposed that this practice on the part of the
newly enfranchised class at the South had been impelled by a dire necessity.
It is a bad practice, and one which cannot be commended in a truly civilized
community, but everything in this world is relative. Assault compels defense.
I shall never ask the colored people to be lambs where the whites insist
upon being wolves, and yet no man shall outdo me in efforts to promote
kindness and good will between the races. But I know there can be no
peace without justice, and hence the sword.

One other thing: I hardly think you are quite just in what you say of the
changed manners of the colored people of South Carolina. It does not seem
to me that their degeneracy is so complete as you describe it to be. Were
you not M. R. Delany, I should say that the man who wrote thus of the
manners of the colored people of South Carolina had taken his place with
the old planters. You certainly cannot be among those of the South who
prefer the lash-inspired manners of the past. I know too well your own

proud and independent spirit, to believe that the manners of an enslaved and oppressed people are more to your taste than those which are born of freedom and independence. ⟨. . .⟩

In conclusion, my dear old friend, let me assure you that I rejoice in every honor of which you are the recipient, and hold you worthy of all that have been bestowed upon you, and of still higher promotion. Let me also assure you of my cordial co-operation with you in all well-directed efforts to elevate and improve our race, to break down all unjust and mischievous distinctions among them, and secure for them a just measure of the political privileges now so largely monopolized by our white fellow-countrymen.

Frederick Douglass, "Letter to Major Delany" (1871), *The Life and Writings of Frederick Douglass*, ed. Philip S. Foner (New York: International Publishers, 1955), Vol. 4, pp. 276–78, 281

JESSIE FAUSET   To few men is the opportunity given to realize themselves completely. What must not have been his supreme joy to know that he, born in an age when color was a misdemeanor to be expiated with life servitude, attained to honors such as many a man born under a more favorable star failed to grasp? Of course, there were in his career moments of despair, even of failure, but in the main his dreams came true. He lived to see himself become a man among men and millions of his fellows elevated from the status of chattels to manhood and citizenship.

Take him all in all and he was as fine an example of self-reliance and courage as any race might hope for. Dr. Delany believed that power came from within; he believed it the duty of the American Negro deliberately to plan his future and not leave it to the whims of fate. Wisdom with understanding expressed the sum total of his admonitions and doubtless he would have added: "Embellish that understanding with pride; commit no actions that can shake it."

⟨. . .⟩ the main lesson bequeathed by his life for his countrymen of a later date was his unshakable pride, the bulwark of his existence, the mainspring of his actions. His blood and his blackness were the insignia of his rank and no gallant of the bravest days of France believed more truly than he that rank imposes obligation,—*noblesse oblige*.

Jessie Fauset, " 'Rank Imposes Obligation,' " *Crisis* 33, No. 1 (November 1926): 12–13

THEODORE DRAPER   Such in brief was the extraordinary life of the founding father of black nationalism in America. Yet the consistently

emigrationist portion of his life filled only about ten years. After 1861 he
went further and further away from the cause to which he owes his fame,
and for almost a quarter of a century he represented reconciliation far more
than emigration. His entire life was filled with contradictions and dualities.
Before the Civil War his achievements would have done honor to any man,
white or black. Yet the fact that Delany was black made it possible for one
of his superior gifts and attainments to advocate fleeing from the land of
his birth. Whatever his rank or profession, he still felt despised and rejected.

But this was only one side of the story, the side that black nationalists
have preferred to remember. The other side was that he never fled very far
from home, and even his sojourn in Canada did not last very long. He went
to Africa as an explorer, not as a settler. Once the Civil War offered some
hope of emancipation, he could not restrain his impulse to throw himself
into the thick of it. Then he more or less made peace with the country
that he once said had bade him begone and had driven him from her
embraces. He preferred to support a moderate white, Wade Hampton, than to
go all the way with the extreme black Reconstructionists and thus indirectly
helped to restore white rule in South Carolina. This was the final contradiction, the ultimate duality in the life and public service of Martin R. Delany.

> Theodore Draper, "The Founder of American Black Nationalism," *New York Review
> of Books*, 12 March 1970, p. 40

VICTOR ULLMAN   Delany was the first to *demand*—not *appeal*—
for black freedom and equality for the very simplest of reasons—because *"I
am a Man."* To hell with justice, which man has never granted, or godliness,
which man has never achieved, or political equality, which always has been
a chimera whether in the guise of democracy or autocracy. Delany demanded
recognition as a member of the human race, in good standing.

Today, such status is called "black pride." It is a total denial of centuries
of weeping over the burden of a black skin. Delany expressed it with his
earliest efforts in Pittsburgh. He fought with other black leaders to adopt
it as an essential element in any black nationalist movement. He could not
forgive any of his fellows—including Frederick Douglass—for their "Uncle
Tomism" in licking the white hand for favors long overdue.

That is why there was no compromise with whites in Delany's make-
up as a man. He had infinite love and compassion, openly demonstrated
paternalism for any and all members of his own race—except those who
had adopted the white man's vices.

There was a duality in him which could either result from egomania or
from the purest integrity. The whites considered it the former and, as one

prominent South Carolina white said: "Sir, I do not believe Delany considers any white man as good as himself."

On the other hand, Delany's pride of race was such as to distinguish him among his fellows and command their slavish following.

Delany's philosophical descendants of today—the black militants—have recently discovered black pride, but he knew it, felt it, demanded it, and defined it to his very first and youthful audiences in Pittsburgh during the 1830s. Throughout the fifty years of service to his people Delany did not deviate from his definition though he did vary his technique of its presentation.

"*I am a Man*" meant solely and exclusively that he *must* enjoy all of the favors or suffer all of the pains of being a man, no matter what his color or physical characteristics. To Delany that was the First Commandment.

It was this unequivocal stand that made enemies and friends, fierce opponents and stalwart followers. It is true that his arrogantly expressed beliefs won over few whites, but it did win the respect of all. And Delany perhaps had a good reason for his militant expression. He had read the ancients and very few of his day, of any color, had done the same. There *had* been great black civilizations.

But such proof and the mere statement "*I am a Man*" was not enough for the color phobia, then or now. Black pride is an empty phrase and becomes a form of separatism without the ingredient of hope. What if there had been mighty and learned black civilizations in Africa? What were the glories of Greece? The entire world needed an inferior race to exploit through colonialism, and the United States needed slavery. That need dictated the inferiority of the blacks, and so a Christian civilization, a modern economy, and a political system called democracy all were perverted in proof that the "nigger" was not a man.

And so Delany called upon the future as well as the past to prove his thesis. He gave his people hope that "*I am a Man*" had concrete meaning by raising the ghost haunting all whites today. During his early writings and speeches Delany seldom failed to tell his black audiences that there was a reality in black pride that the almost immediate future would prove. He said it in many ways but perhaps most succinctly at his Emigration Convention in Cleveland in 1854:

> The white race are but one-third of the population of the globe—
> or one of them to two of us—and it cannot much longer continue
> that two-thirds will passively submit to the universal domination
> of this one-third. . . .

Here was the fact to buttress the wish expression of black pride. It was a future in keeping with the past shown by Delany to his people. It was hope for the blacks.

Victor Ullman, *Martin R. Delany: The Beginnings of Black Nationalism* (Boston: Beacon Press, 1971), pp. 516–18

RONALD TAKAKI   The land of black redemption ⟨in *Blake*⟩ is Africa. Thus the revolutionary struggle of Blake and his friends focuses ultimately on the fatherland. An important element of the revolution as Blake defines it is the accumulation of money. Thus he tells his fellow black revolutionaries that they must have money in order to obtain their freedom. "With money you may effect your escape almost at any time. Your most difficult point is an elevated obstruction, a mighty hill, a mountain; but through that hill there is a gap; and *money* is the passport through that *White Gap* to freedom. . . . Money alone will carry you through the White mountains or across the White river to liberty." Later in the novel, it becomes clear that the *"White Gap"* is related to the regeneration of Africa. In a conversation between two of Blake's fellow revolutionaries in Cuba, Madame Cordora and Placido, the significance of black enterprise in Africa as a basis of black redemption is made explicit. Placido, the thoughtful poet of the revolution, explains that images of Africa as a land of lazy and savage people have buttressed notions of black inferiority and have allowed whites to regard blacks as incapable of civilization and fit only to be slaves. Once blacks prove that in "Africa their native land, they are among the most industrious people in the world, highly cultivating the lands, and that ere long they and their country must hold the balance of commercial power by supplying . . . the greatest staple commodities in demand," they would be respected in the world. There are, Placido adds, "undoubted probabilities" that Africa could become a great commercial country. And Madame Cordora, a wealthy mulatto lady involved in Blake's revolution, suddenly realizes the meaning of the struggle and its relationship to African nationalism. "I never before felt as proud of my black as I did of my white blood," she joyfully exclaims. "I can readily see that the blacks compose an important element in the commercial and social relations of the world." Clearly black psychological as well as political liberation depends on the success of black economic enterprise within the framework of building a black nation in Africa, the "native land" of blacks everywhere.

Ronald Takaki, "War upon the Whites: Black Rage in the Fiction of Martin Delany," *Violence in the Black Imagination* (New York: Putnam's, 1972), p. 97

ROGER W. HITE   Delany's rhetorical design ⟨in *Blake*⟩ argues that *Christianity and slavery*, not religion and revolution, are incompatible concepts. Whereas Henry symbolizes the possibility of the latter, a description of a slave sale ironically illustrates the absurdity of the former. Delany describes a situation where just as the auctioneer shouts out "Who'll give me one thousand five," a sudden thundershower threatens to cancel the sale. The day is saved by an anonymous "gentleman" who makes his way through the crowd and informs the auctioneer that "those concerned had kindly tendered the use of the church which stood nearby, in which to continue the sale." Selling human flesh in the house of the Lord—a bitter attack on the insensitivity of ante-bellum Christians to the evils of slavery.

The novel constantly underscores the inconsistency of good Christians, "elders in the Church," who without wincing wreck black bodies and sever families on the auction block. Perhaps the most grotesque and outrageous illustration of this "Christian" insensitivity is a scene Delany paints of a small boy who vomits blood and dies after a severe whipping administered because an illness prevented him from behaving like a dog and performing circus tricks to satisfy onlooking white spectators. ⟨. . .⟩

Delany used the novel as a vehicle for attacking institutions which seemed to foster oppression of black Americans. Frequently the dialogue is reduced to monologue as Henry expounds Delany's own political analysis: an analysis which underscored the belief that Christianity and slavery, not religion and revolution, were antithetical. Henry becomes Delany's vehicle for preaching a message urging blacks to reevaluate the worth of Christianity as practiced by whites and taught to slaves. Henry's evolution seems almost prophetic as he symbolizes the black man who rejects the white man's religion, only to emerge as a black messiah in his own right. One can only remain curious as to how Delany might have reacted to the modern Muslim movement. We find in *Blake* the same mixture of black nationalism and anti-white religious sentiments reflected in the words and deeds of modern black leaders such as Malcolm X and Elijah Muhammad.

Roger W. Hite, " 'Stand Still and See the Salvation': The Rhetorical Design of Martin Delany's *Blake*," *Journal of Black Studies* 5, No. 2 (December 1947): 196, 201

CYRIL E. GRIFFITH   Delany's monograph ⟨*The Principia of Ethnology*⟩ was really a literary supplement to his earlier polemical essay, and an effort to add "new" evidence to his thesis that Africans were the first civilized men. In the latest work, however, Delany contended that there was a definite link between human creation and African civilization. He believed all races evolved from one human ancestor, but God employed three agencies to disperse man throughout the earth and to foster the development of diverse civilizations. These agencies were "Revolution, Conquest, and Emigration." For him, emigration was the most essential agent because it placed men in various geographical regions where they initiated progressive revolutions. Delany admitted there were violent revolutions, but he preferred nonviolent revolutions to promote civilization. The Tower of Babel and the Great Flood were catastrophic events designed to make man migrate from his original homeland. The deluge was significant because it caused the Hamitic migration into the northeastern region of the African continent. In his essay Delany doubted the European view of outside influences on Africa, but in his book he expressed no reservations about the Hamitic migration into Africa. He claimed that the Hamites were negroid, not caucasoid. They were among the ancestors of those ancient Africans who had built "imperishable monuments of their superior attainments" in Egypt, Sudan, and Ethiopia.

Toward the end of the book Delany suggested that it was important for contemporary blacks to recognize and appreciate the achievements of the ancient Africans. The Egyptians, Sudanese, and Ethiopians had reached a high stage of development because of the stability of their cultures. In modern times, however, Delany feared that continual white influences on black men everywhere would result in the cultural decay of the race. West Africans near the coast were corrupted already by their associations with Europeans, but people in the interior had maintained the traditional life style of their ancestors. Yet a growing European presence on the continent appeared imminent. Culturally, Delany felt that the future appeared bleak for new world blacks because acculturation and miscegenation greatly had diminished their African identity. The pan-African leader admitted that Africans had fallen behind Europeans in modern times. But a new initiative by black men in the motherland and the diaspora would assure the regeneration of the race, and the theories about racial inferiority could not prevent its upward mobility.

> Cyril E. Griffith, *The African Dream: Martin R. Delany and the Emergence of Pan-African Thought* (University Park: Pennsylvania State University Press, 1975), pp. 105–6

KRISTIN HERZOG   Two qualities differentiate Blake from a black Jewish-Christian prophet and leader like Harriet Beecher Stowe's Dred. One is his rationalism, the other—to put it anachronistically—is his quasi-

Marxism. Some of his statements express an eighteenth-century rationalistic understanding of nature and the Deity combined with a revolutionary romanticism: "Equality of rights in Nature's plan, / To follow nature is the march of man." The general insurrection which Henry Holland envisions will be as natural as "the whistling of the wind, rustling of the leaves, flashing of lightning, roaring of thunder, and running of streams." Historical change is as inevitable as the flux of Nature: "That time to strike was fast verging upon them, from which, like the approach of the evening shadow of the hilltops, there was no escape." Henry's rationalism is also obvious when he becomes a High Conjurer in the Dismal Swamp. He is eager to "enlighten" his friends on his position that conjuring is a foolish superstition which simply puts money in the conjurer's pocket and makes the slaves passive and dependent. He becomes a conjurer only as a means of being all things to all people, because "I'll do anything not morally wrong, to gain our freedom; and to effect this, we must take the slaves, not as we wish them to be, but as we really find them to be." What Blake considers "morally wrong," however, is not dependent on traditional morality. "I'm incapable of stealing from anyone, but I have, from time to time, taken by littles, some of the earnings due me for more than eighteen years service to this man Franks, which at the low rate of two hundred dollars a year, would amount to sixteen hundred dollars more than I secured, exclusive of the interest, which would have more than supplied my clothing, to say nothing of the injury done me by degrading me as a slave." He exhorts the slaves to keep the overriding issue of economics in mind. "God told the Egyptian slaves to 'borrow from their neighbours'—meaning their oppressors—'all their jewels'—meaning to take their money and wealth wherever they could lay hands upon it, and depart from Egypt. So you must teach them to take all the money they can get from their masters to enable them to make the strike without a failure." On the flight north, any white ferryman can be bribed with money. "Delany departs radically from the Abolitionist formula of broken families and violated octoroons by treating slavery primarily as an exploitative labor system. It is a remarkable novel, closer in spirit to Karl Marx than to the New England Abolitionists" ⟨Robert Bone⟩.

Kristin Herzog, "Martin R. Delany's *Blake*: Resistance and Aggression in Women and Slaves," *Women, Ethnics, and Exotics: Images of Power in Mid-Nineteenth-Century American Fiction* (Knoxville: University of Tennessee Press, 1983), pp. 154–55

MELVIN B. RAHMING   ⟨. . .⟩ the issues which were woven into the fabric of debate in the eighteenth and nineteenth centuries were Pan-Africanism, its attendant phenomena (black nationalism and emigrationism) and its opposite (integration). It is against this ideological back-ground that the revolutionary activities of Delany's protagonist (in *Blake*) have their relevance and that the implications of Delany's West Indian portrait are best understood.

In the figure of Henry Blake, Delany embodies, somewhat unevenly, representative criteria of the three alternatives (Pan-Africanism, black nationalism, and emigrationism) and argues passionately against the fourth (integration). Henry is Delany's statement to white-directed emigration organizations like the American Colonization Society that the black Ameri-can's journey to Africa has to begin with the black psyche; that emigration to Africa will be culturally useless if it is not motivated and directed by black people who are psychologically divorced from a white value system and who define the nature and dictate the course of their own humanity. So it is that Henry encourages the emigration of rebellious slaves to Canada and solicits no aid from white-directed organizations. So it is also that Henry reverses the black-white Anglo-European system of aesthetics. His epithets for the white race—"candlefaces," "alabasters"—are as negative as the mod-ern word "honky." When Henry says "I now declare war against our oppres-sors," he is speaking both literally and metaphorically. He is adamantly opposed to the idea that slaves should adopt the values of their white masters, and he knows that his pure black body is synonymous with manhood and strength and that it should be the physical evidence of a psycho-cultural blackness. The only way for the black race in America to ensure this union of body and mind, Henry believes, is to reject everything which perpetuates feelings of inadequacy and inferiority within and about black people. Such psycho-cultural debunking is the very soul of Delany's Pan-Africanism. The organizing and politicizing of this frame of mind becomes Henry's task—he must assist the eventual institution of a lifestyle which would de-Europe-anize the black mentality.

Melvin B. Rahming, "Martin Delany's *Blake* and the Historical Background," *The Evolution of the West Indian's Image in the Afro-American Novel* (Millwood, NY: Associated Faculty Press, 1986), pp. 13–14

48

◈ *Bibliography*

Elegy on the Life and Character of the Rev. Fayette Davis. 1847.

The Condition, Elevation, Emigration, and Destiny of the Colored People of the United States: Politically Considered. 1852.

The Origin and Objects of Ancient Freemasonry; Its Introduction into the United States, and Legitimacy among Colored Men. 1853.

Official Report of the Niger Valley Exploring Party. 1861.

University Pamphlets: A Series of Four Tracts on National Policy. 1870.

Homes for the Freedmen. 1871.

Principia of Ethnology: The Origin of Races and Color, with an Archeological Compendium of Ethiopian and Egyptian Civilization, from Years of Careful Examination and Enquiry. 1879.

Blake; or, The Huts of America. 1970.

Frederick Douglass
1818–1895

FREDERICK DOUGLASS was born into slavery in February 1818 on a plantation in Maryland. The exact date of his birth and the identity of his father were never known to him. Though Douglass knew his mother, Harriet Bailey, he had little contact with her. He eluded the demands of slavery and lived in relative happiness with his maternal grandmother Betsey Bailey until 1824, when he was forced by his master Aaron Anthony to serve the Lloyd family, from whom Anthony rented a farm. On that day, he claims, his childhood ended. Douglass was introduced to the horrors of slavery during this period, as well as the ostentatious wealth of the Lloyd family. Douglass was the companion of Colonel Lloyd's son, Daniel, until 1826 when he was sent to Baltimore to serve the Auld family, in-laws of Aaron Anthony, where he became the companion of the Auld's newborn son, Thomas. Douglass also received the tutelage of Sophia Auld, who began to teach him how to read and write until forbidden to do so by her husband.

From 1827 to 1832 Douglass, who became the property of Thomas Auld upon the death of Aaron Anthony in 1826, remained with Hugh and Sophia Auld. During this time he continued to educate himself, met free blacks, and read abolitionist newspapers. He also helplessly watched the Aulds separate his family, selling many members south. Thomas Auld, discouraged by Douglass's worsening disposition, sent him to a slave breaker named Edward Covey. Douglass endured the worst of slavery—the fields and the whip—until he could stand no more and wrestled Covey for his dignity. His will strengthened by the victory over Covey, Douglass planned an escape. The escape, however, was discovered, and Douglass was returned to the Aulds.

From 1836 to 1838 Douglass worked as an apprentice ship caulker. His life around the docks brought him into contact with the outside world again, renewing his hope for freedom. On September 3, 1838, Douglass, in the guise of a sailor, boarded a train and rode without incident to the free states. Shortly thereafter, on September 15, he married Anna Murray, a free black woman from Baltimore. The couple moved from New York City to New Bedford, Massachusetts, where Douglass was invited by the prominent abolitionist William Lloyd Garrison to recount his life as a slave at abolitionist meetings. Douglass revealed a natural ability for oratory and became a powerful abolitionist speaker. Douglass's eloquence, in fact, caused many audiences to doubt that he was once a slave. In 1845, to substantiate his biographical speeches, he published *Narrative of the Life of Frederick Douglass, an American Slave: Written by Himself*. In exposing his identity, circumstances, and former owner, he exposed himself to recapture and therefore fled to Great Britain, where he continued speaking for the abolitionist cause while his book became a best-seller in Europe and America. Money was raised by his English friends to purchase his freedom, and in 1847 he returned to America as a freeman. Douglass began publishing a newspaper, the *North Star* (renamed *Frederick Douglass' Paper* in 1851), in which he published his only known work of fiction, "The Heroic Slave." In 1855 he published a revised edition of his autobiography entitled *My Bondage and My Freedom*, which was also well received, and still another version in 1881 entitled *Life and Times of Frederick Douglass*. Many of the speeches Douglass delivered over his long career as public speaker were published as pamphlets. These and his other writings were assembled by Philip S. Foner in *The Life and Writings of Frederick Douglass* (5 vols., 1950–75). A new edition of his works, under the title *The Frederick Douglass Papers*, is now being compiled under the editorship of John W. Blassingame.

In his later years Douglass received several political appointments: assistant secretary of the Santo Domingo Comission (1871), president of the Freedman's Bank (1874), marshall (1874–81) and recorder of deeds (1881–86) of the District of Columbia, and U.S. minister to Haiti (1889–91). He died on February 20, 1895, after attending a woman's suffrage meeting.

🞖 *Critical Extracts*

WILLIAM LLOYD GARRISON   Mr. Douglass has very properly chosen to write his own Narrative, in his own style, and according to the best of his ability, rather than to employ someone else. It is, therefore, entirely his own production; and, considering how long and dark was the career he had to run as a slave,—how few have been his opportunities to improve his mind since he broke his iron fetters,—it is, in my judgement, highly creditable to his head and heart. He who can peruse without a tearful eye, a heaving breast, and afflicted spirit,—without being filled with an unutterable abhorrence of slavery and all its abettors, and animated with a determination to seek the immediate overthrow of that execrable system,— without trembling for the fate of his country in the hands of a righteous God, who is ever on the side of the oppressed, and whose arm is not shortened that it can not save,—must have a flinty heart, and be qualified to act the part of a trafficker "in slaves and the souls of men." I am confident that it is essentially true in all its statements; that nothing has been set down in malice, nothing exaggerated, nothing drawn from the imagination; that it comes short of the reality, rather than overstates a single fact in regard to SLAVERY AS IT IS. The experience of Frederick Douglass, as a slave, was not a peculiar one; his lot was not especially a hard one; his case may be regarded as a very fair specimen of the treatment of slaves in Maryland, in which state it is conceded that they are better fed and less cruelly treated than in Georgia, Alabama, or Louisiana. Many have suffered incomparably more, while very few on the plantations have suffered less, than himself. Yet how deplorable was his situation! what terrible chastise- ments were inflicted upon his person! what still more shocking outrages were perpetrated on his mind! with all his noble powers and sublime aspira- tions, how like a brute was he treated, even by those professing to have the same mind in them that was in Jesus Christ! to what dreadful liabilities was he continually subjected! how destitute of friendly counsel and aid, even in his greatest extremities! how heavy was the midnight of woe which shrouded in blackness the last ray of hope, and filled the future with terror and gloom! what longings after freedom took possession of his breast, and how misery augmented, in proportion as he grew reflective and intelligent,— thus demonstrating that a happy slave is an extinct man! how he thought, reasoned, felt, under the lash of the driver, with the chains upon his limbs! what perils he encountered in his endeavors to escape from his horrible doom! and how signal have been his deliverance and preservation in the midst of a nation of pitiless enemies!

William Lloyd Garrison, "Preface," *Narrative of the Life of Frederick Douglass, an American Slave: Written by Himself* (1845; rpt. Harmondsworth: Penguin, 1982), pp. 37–39

FREDERICK DOUGLASS   I have been frequently asked how I felt when I found myself in a free State. I have never been able to answer the question with any satisfaction to myself. It was a moment of the highest excitement I ever experienced. I suppose I felt as one may imagine the unarmed mariner to feel when he is rescued by a friendly man-of-war from the pursuit of a pirate. In writing to a dear friend, immediately after my arrival at New York, I said I felt like one who had escaped a den of hungry lions. This state of mind, however, very soon subsided; and I was again seized with a feeling of great insecurity and loneliness. I was yet liable to be taken back, and subjected to all the tortures of slavery. This in itself was enough to damp the ardor of my enthusiasm. But the loneliness overcame me. There I was in the midst of thousands, and yet a perfect stranger; without home and without friends, in the midst of thousands of my own brethren—children of a common Father, and yet I dared not to unfold to any of them my sad condition. I was afraid to speak to any one for fear of speaking to the wrong one, and thereby falling into the hands of money-loving kidnappers, whose business it was to lie in wait for the panting fugitive, as the ferocious beasts of the forest lie in wait for their prey. The motto which I adopted when I started from slavery was this—"Trust no man!" I saw in every white man an enemy, and in almost every colored man cause for distrust. It was a most painful situation; and, to understand it, one must needs experience it, or imagine himself in similar circumstances. Let him be a fugitive slave in a strange land—a land given up to be the hunting-ground for slaveholders—whose inhabitants are legalized kidnappers—where he is every moment subjected to the terrible liability of being seized upon by his fellow-men, as the hideous crocodile seizes upon his prey!—I say, let him place himself in my situation—without home or friends—without money or credit—wanting shelter, and no one to give it—wanting bread, and no money to buy it,—and at the same time let him feel that he is pursued by merciless men-hunters, and in total darkness as to what to do, where to go, or where to stay,—perfectly helpless both as to the means of defence and means of escape,—in the midst of plenty, yet suffering the terrible gnawings of hunger,—in the midst of houses, yet having no home,—among fellow-men, yet feeling as if in the midst of wild beasts, whose greediness to swallow up the trembling and half-famished fugitive is only equalled by that with which the monsters of the deep swallow up the helpless fish upon which they subsist,—I say, let him be placed in this most trying situation,—the situation in which I was placed,—then, and not till then, will he fully appreciate the hardships of, and know how to sympathize with, the toil-worn and whip-scarred fugitive slave.

Frederick Douglass, *Narrative of the Life of Frederick Douglass, an American Slave: Written by Himself* (1845; rpt. Harmondsworth: Penguin, 1982), pp. 143–44

CHARLES W. CHESNUTT   Douglass possessed in unusual degree
the faculty of swaying his audience, sometimes against their maturer judgment. There is something in the argument from first principles which, if
presented with force and eloquence, never fails to appeal to those who are
not blinded by self-interest or deep-seated prejudice. Douglass's argument
was that of the Declaration of Independence,—"that *all* men are created
equal; that they are endowed by their Creator with certain inalienable rights;
that among these are life, liberty, and the pursuit of happiness. That, to
secure these rights, governments are instituted among men, deriving their
just powers from the *consent of the governed.*" The writer may be pardoned
for this quotation; for there are times when we seem to forget that now and
here, no less than in ancient Rome, "eternal vigilance is the price of liberty."
Douglass brushed aside all sophistries about Constitutional guarantees, and
vested rights, and inferior races, and, having postulated the right of men
to be free, maintained that negroes were men, and offered himself as a proof
of his assertion,—an argument that few had the temerity to deny. If it were
answered that he was only half a negro, he would reply that slavery made
no such distinction, and as a still more irrefutable argument would point
to his friend, Samuel R. Ward, who often accompanied him on the platform,—an eloquent and effective orator, of whom Wendell Phillips said
that "he was so black that, if he would shut his eyes, one could not see
him." It was difficult for an auditor to avoid assent to such arguments,
presented with all the force and fire of genius, relieved by a ready wit, a
contagious humor, and a tear-compelling power rarely excelled.

Charles W. Chesnutt, *Frederick Douglass* (Boston: Small, Maynard, 1899), pp. 110–11

ARNA BONTEMPS   It was a daring thing to attempt. Perhaps it
was even reckless, but by now Douglass had considered and rejected every
alternative. To answer those people who had begun to doubt his story, to
silence the whispering that threatened to destroy his value as an abolitionist
agent, he would throw caution away, he would put the full account in
writing. That was it. He would write a *book.* In his book he would tell the
whole world just whose slave he had been, how he had squirmed and plotted
in his chains, where and when he had escaped. The only detail he would
withhold would be the manner of his getaway. Even that would not be
concealed for his own sake. He would reveal everything and take his chances
as a fugitive in Massachusetts. But to disclose the maneuver by which he
gave his owners the slip would be to close that particular gate to other
slaves. That he would not do. As for the rest, the lid was off. Next time

he undertook a series of lectures, he would have an answer for those who accused him of inventing personal history for the sake of winning antislavery sympathizers.

> Arna Bontemps, *Free at Last: The Life of Frederick Douglass* (New York: Dodd, Mead, 1971), p. 95

ROBERT B. STEPTO   One reason Douglass wrote 'The Heroic Slave' is easy to come by. In 1845, in response to the taunting cries that he had never been a slave, Douglass was 'induced', as he put it ⟨in *My Bondage and My Freedom*⟩, 'to write out the leading facts connected with [his] experience in slavery, giving names of persons, places, and dates—thus putting it in the power of any who doubted, to ascertain the truth or falsehood of [his] story of being a fugitive slave'. Thus *The Narrative of the Life of Frederick Douglass, an American Slave, Written by Himself* came to life. And in 1847, while harassed by suggestions that his *place* was to speak, not to write, Douglass began the *North Star*, his mission being to demonstrate that a 'tolerably well conducted press, in the hands of persons of the despised race', could prove to be a 'most powerful means of removing prejudice, and of awakening an interest in them'. Then, in 1852, Douglass took a logical next step: he wrote a historical fiction about a heroic slave named Madison Washington who had led a slave revolt aboard a slave ship in 1841. All these *writing* activities, as opposed to speaking duties, are of a piece, each one bolder than the one preceding it, each a measure of Douglass's remove from acts of literacy involving merely spoken renditions of what Garrison and company alternately called Douglass's 'facts' or 'story' or simply 'narrative'. This suggests something of why Douglass would attempt a novella at this time ⟨. . .⟩

'The Heroic Slave' is not an altogether extraordinary piece of work. I'm not about to argue that it should take a place beside, say, *Benito Cereno* as a major short fiction of the day. Still, after dismissing the florid soliloquies which unfortunately besmirch this and too many other anti-slavery writings, we find that the novella is full of craft, especially of the sort that combines artfulness with a certain fabulistic usefulness. Appropriately enough, evidence of Douglass's craft is available in the novella's attention to both theme and character. In Part I of 'The Heroic Slave' we are told of the 'double state' of Virginia and introduced not only to Madison Washington but also to Mr Listwell, who figures as the model abolitionist in the story. The meticulous development of the Virginia theme and of the portrait of

Mr Listwell, much more than the portrayal of Washington as a hero, is the stuff of useful art-making in Douglass's novella.

The theme of the duality or 'doubleness' of Virginia begins in the novella's very first sentence: 'The State of Virginia is famous in American annals for the multitudinous array of her statesmen and heroes.' The rest of the paragraph continues as follows:

> She has been dignified by some the mother of statesmen.
> History has not been sparing in recording their names, or in blazoning
> their deeds. Her high position in this respect, has given her
> enviable distinction among her sister States. With Virginia
> for his birth-place, even a man of ordinary parts, on account of
> the general partiality for her sons, easily rises to eminent
> stations. Men, not great enough to attract attention in their
> native States, have, like a certain distinguished citizen in
> the State of New York, sighed and repined that they were not
> born in Virginia. Yet not all the great ones of the Old
> Dominion have, by the fact of their birthplace, escaped
> undeserved obscurity. By some strange neglect, *one* of the
> truest, manliest, and bravest of her children,—one who, in after
> years, will, I think, command the pen of genius to set his
> merits forth—holds now no higher place in the records of that
> grand old Commonwealth than is held by a horse or an ox.
> Let those account for it who can, but there stands the fact, that
> a man who loved liberty as well as did Patrick Henry—who
> deserved it as much as Thomas Jefferson—and who fought for
> it with a valor as high, an arm as strong, and against odds
> as great as he who led all the armies of the American colonies
> through the great war for freedom and independence, lives
> now only in the chattel records of his native state.

At least two features here are worthy of note. The paragraph as a whole, but especially its initial sentences, can be seen as significant revoicing of the conventional opening of a slave narrative. Slave narratives usually begin with the phrase 'I was born'; this is true of Douglass's 1845 *Narrative* and true also, as James Olney reminds us, of the narratives of Henry Bibb, Henry 'Box' Brown, William Wells Brown, John Thompson, Samuel Ringgold Ward, James W. C. Pennington, Austin Steward, James Roberts, and many, many other former slaves. In 'The Heroic Slave', however, Douglass transforms 'I was born' into the broader assertion that in Virginia many heroes have been born. After that, he then works his way to the central point that a certain *one*—an unknown hero who lives now only in the chattel records and not the history books—has been born. Douglass knows the slave-narrative convention, partly because he has used it himself; but, more to the point, he seems to have an understanding of how to exploit its rhetorical usefulness in terms of proclaiming the existence and identity of an individual without merely employing it verbatim. This is clear evidence, I think, of a first step, albeit a small one, toward the creation of an Afro-American fiction based upon the conventions of the slave narratives. That Douglass himself was quite possibly thinking in these terms while writing is suggested by his persistent reference to the 'chattel records' which must, in effect, be transformed by 'the pen of genius' so that his hero's merits may be set forth—indeed, set free. If by this Douglass means that his hero's story must be liberated from the realm—the text—of brutal fact and, more, that texts must be created to compete with other texts, then it's safe to say that he brought to the creation of 'The Heroic Slave' all the intentions, if not all the skills, of the self-conscious *writer*.

Robert B. Stepto, "Storytelling in Early Afro-American Fiction: Frederick Douglass's 'The Heroic Slave,' " *Black Literature and Literary Theory*, ed. Henry Louis Gates, Jr. (New York: Methuen, 1984) pp. 177–80

WALDO E. MARTIN, JR.   In many ways, Frederick Douglass remains the prototypical black American hero: a peerless self-made man and symbol of success; a fearless and tireless spokesman; a thoroughgoing humanist. The most striking and enduring aspect of Douglass's heroic legacy in his day—its classic, even archetypal aura—has persisted down to the present. Although often viewed and used differently by others, the heroic and legendary Douglass clearly personifies the American success ethic. The key to his eminently evocative essence is twofold. First, he, like the American nation itself and its most enduring folk heroes, rose above seemingly overwhelming odds to achieve historical distinction. Second, he represents a model self-made man: an exemplary black version of uncommon achievement primarily through the agency of a resolute will and hard toil aided by moral law and divine providence. Not only did he succeed, but he did so in terms signifying mythic greatness: the uniquely gifted individual rising above anonymity and adversity to renown and good fortune largely through the force of superlative character and indefatigable effort. Douglass's life story exemplifies both the romance and the reality of heroic greatness.

Notwithstanding its universal appeal, Douglass's heroic and symbolic viability has had special meaning for black Americans. In 1908, Kelly Miller, Howard University sociologist and mathematician, gave his view of Douglass's particular importance for black Americans. "Frederick Douglass is the one commanding historic character of the colored race in America. He is the model of emulation of those who are struggling up through the trials and difficulties which he himself suffered and subdued. He is illustrative and exemplary of what they might become—the first fruit of promise of a dormant race. To the aspiring colored youth of this land Mr. Douglass is, at once, the inspiration of their hopes and the justification of their claims." While one may reasonably argue, especially today, with Miller's claim of Douglass's singular historical eminence, his claim for Douglass's prototypical heroic and symbolic preeminence is more cogent. Perhaps better than any other nineteenth-century black American, Douglass personified the travail and triumph of his people. A heroic and symbolic view of Douglass continues to be meaningful because his life struggle so vividly represented his people's struggle. In 1853, he remarked that "mine has been the experience of the colored people of America, both slave and free." Douglass saw himself and wanted to be seen as an example and an inspiration to all people, but especially to blacks.

Waldo E. Martin, Jr., *The Mind of Frederick Douglass* (Chapel Hill: University of North Carolina Press, 1984), p. 253

JOHN SEKORA   Because it is one of the most important books ever published in America, Frederick Douglass's *Narrative* of 1845 has justly received much attention. That attention has been increasing for a generation at a rate parallel to the growth in interest in autobiography as a literary genre, and the *Narrative* as autobiography has been the subject of several influential studies. Without denying the insights of such studies, I should like to suggest that in 1845 Douglass had no opportunity to write what (since the eighteenth century) we would call autobiography, that the achievement of the *Narrative* lies in another form. ⟨. . .⟩

The *Narrative*, I would contend, is the first comprehensive, personal history of American slavery. Autobiography would come a decade later, in *My Bondage and My Freedom*. If many readers prefer the earlier volume, the reasons are not so far to search. The *Narrative* is as tightly written as a sonnet, the work of years in the pulpit and on the lecture circuit. It comprehends all major aspects of slavery as Douglass knew it in a narrative that is as dramatically compassing as any first-person novel. It is at the same time a personal history of the struggle with and for language—against words that repress, for words that liberate. It is for author and reader alike a personalizing account of a system that would depersonalize everyone. It is the retelling of the most important Christian story, the Crucifixion, in the midst of the most important American civil crisis, the battle over slavery.

In *The Fugitive Blacksmith* ⟨James W. C.⟩ Pennington asked if a slave had no need of character. He answered the question in the following way: "Suppose insult, reproach, or slander, should render it necessary for him to appeal to the history of his family in vindication of his character, where does he find that history? He goes to his native state, to his native county, to his native town; but nowhere does he find any record of himself *as a man.*" It is an acute question, one he is eager to raise, I believe, because of Douglass's example. Douglass renewed the conservative form of the slave narrative at a critical time. He gave record of himself as an antislavery man. And the magnitude of that achievement is difficult to overestimate. For in moral terms the slave narrative and its postbellum heirs are the only history of American slavery we have. Outside the narrative, slavery was a wordless, nameless, timeless time. It was time without history and time with imminence. Slaveholders sought to reduce existence to the duration of the psychological present and to mandate their records as the only reliable texts. Whatever the restrictions placed upon them, Douglass and the other narrators changed that forever. To recall one's personal history is to *renew* it. The *Narrative* is both instrument and inscription of that renewal.

John Sekora, "Comprehending Slavery: Language and Personal History in Douglass's *Narrative* of 1845," *CLA Journal* 29, No. 2 (December 1985): 157–58, 169–70

BLYDEN JACKSON   In terms of content, Douglass' *Narrative* abounds with episodes which are nothing more or less than case studies illustrative of the inhumanity of slavery to the slave and of this very slave's humanity in spite of his inhuman treatment by southern, and many northern, whites and in obvious contradiction to such pseudoscientists as Dr. Josiah Nott of Mobile, who would, by 1850, deny that blacks and whites even belonged to the same genus of the animal kingdom. Atrocities are committed, in the *Narrative*, as far as, allegedly, in at least five cases, the extreme of cold-blooded murder, by whites upon blacks. No atrocities are committed there in any way by negroes. Black women are preyed upon sexually, in the *Narrative*, by white men. Of course, no white women in the *Narrative* are subjected to the venery of black men. And while the slaves in the *Narrative* live meanly—poorly housed, poorly clothed, and poorly fed—instance after instance of their unquenchable propensity to care for one another in the role of a responsible parent or a grateful child or a loyal friend and to observe, in general, an especially magnanimous version of the golden rule toward all their fellow men, demonstrates their ability to rise above their circumstances and to practice those domestic and civic virtues which are the basic underpinnings of a human society in an advanced stage of man's elevation of himself from savagery. One thing more of special note appears in the *Narrative*, a series of pictures revealing the hypocrisy of white southern Christianity. Douglass' voice in the *Narrative* is never more charged with condemnation, contempt, and ire than when he shows some of his white neighbors at worship and then moves on to add, as tellingly as possible, vignettes of these same white neighbors, with their psalms and scriptures still ringing in their supposedly pious ears, abusing their slaves unmercifully. His voice in this regard is a voice found in all other abolitionist slave narratives, just as the case studies of slaves and their masters which supply the content of his *Narrative* are but duplicates of similar case studies distributed copiously throughout all other abolitionist slave narratives.

Once, however, Douglass' acquiescence in the habitual practices of writers associated with the abolitionist slave narrative is recognized, acknowledgement should then be made of what he does which, in his *Narrative*, redeems his resort to those practices from a mere hackneyed reproduction of a prevailing fashion. And what he does thereby constitutes a genuine tribute to his own original powers and his individual cultural growth. He pours, as it were, into old bottles representative of the customs to which he is deferring a fresh and often delightful vintage compounded from the effects directly attributable to aesthetic sensibilities which were his and his alone. As an orator he had held live audiences spellbound, not simply because of his appearance, much to the advantage of any public figure as that appearance was, or of his voice, a rich bass-baritone which he could inflect at will and project, without artificial aid, into the ears of hearers on the farther edge of the not infrequently large crowds that he addressed. But he was, sometimes while he spoke, among other things, a superb mime. He liked, for example, occasionally to turn his platform into a pulpit from which a southern white preacher, a lackey of the slaveholding South, could be seen and heard preaching to slaves, warning them to obey their masters and brandishing over their heads, like a would-be fiery sword, gospel verses in defense of slavery. When he became this preacher, an organic mixture of the real thing and of broad caricature, Douglass was availing himself of talents in his possession which a literary artist might well exactly so have used. It was of these same talents, involving, as they did, a genuinely artistic apprehension, re-creation, and enhancement of reality, that Douglass availed himself in his *Narrative*.

Blyden Jackson, *A History of Afro-American Literature* (Baton Rouge: Louisiana State University Press, 1989), Vol. 1, pp. 111–12

◼ *Bibliography*

Narrative of the Life of Frederick Douglass, an American Slave: Written by Himself.
    1845.

Abolition Fanaticism in New York: Speech of a Runaway Slave from Baltimore,
    at an Abolition Meeting in New York, Held May 11, 1847. 1847.

Farewell Speech, Previously to Embarking on Board the Cambria, upon His Return
    to America. 1847.

Letter to His Old Master. c. 1848.

Lectures on American Slavery. 1851.

Oration Delivered in Corinthian Hall, Rochester. 1852.

Arguments: Pro and Con, on the Case for a National Emigration Convention
    (with W. J. Watkins and J. M. Whitfield). 1854.

The Claims of the Negro Ethnologically Considered. 1854.

My Bondage and My Freedom. 1855.

Address Delivered at the Erection of the Wing Monument, at Mexico, Oswego,
    N.Y., September 11th, 1855. 1855.

The Anti-Slavery Monument: A Lecture Before the Rochester Ladies' Anti-Slavery
    Society. 1855.

Two Speeches. 1857.

Eulogy of the Late Hon. Wm. Jay. 1859.

The Constitution of the United States: Is It Pro-Slavery or Anti-Slavery? c. 1860.

Men of Color, to Arms! 1863.

Addresses at a Mass Meeting . . . for the Promotion of Colored Enlistments (with
    W. D. Kelley and Anna E. Dickinson). 1863.

The Equality of All Men Before the Law Claimed and Defended (with others).
    1865.

U. S. Grant and the Colored People. 1872.

Address Delivered at the Third Annual Fair of the Tennessee Colored Agricultural
    and Mechanical Association. 1873.

Oration Delivered on the Occasion of the Unveiling of the Freedmen's Monument
    in Memory of Abraham Lincoln. 1876.

Speech on the Death of William Lloyd Garrison. c. 1879.

Life and Times of Frederick Douglass. 1881.

John Brown: An Address. 1881.

Address Delivered in the Congregational Church, Washington, D.C., April 16,
    1883: On the Twenty-first Anniversary of Emancipation in the District of
    Columbia. 1883.

⟨*Address to*⟩ *National Convention of Colored Men, at Louisville, Ky., September*
    24, 1883. 1883.

Proceedings of the Civil Rights Mass-Meeting Held in Lincoln Hall, Oct. 22, 1883
    (with Robert G. Ingersoll). 1883.

*Three Addresses on the Relations Subsisting Between the White and Colored People
    of the United States.* 1886.

*The Nation's Problem: A Speech, Delivered Before the Bethel Literary and Historical
    Society.* 1889.

The Race Problem. 1890.

Lecture on Haiti. 1893.

*The Reason Why the Colored American Is Not in the World's Columbian Exposi-
    tion.* 1893.

*Address Delivered in the Metropolitan A.M.E. Church, Washington, D.C., Tues-
    day, January 9th, 1894, on the Lessons of the Hour.* 1894.

A Defence of the Negro Race. 1894.

Why Is the Negro Lynched? 1895.

Negroes and the War Effort. 1942.

Selections from His Writings. Ed. Philip S. Foner. 1945.

Life and Writings. Ed. Philip S. Foner. 1950–75. 5 vols.

Frederick Douglass on Women's Rights. Ed. Philip S. Foner. 1976.

*A Black Diplomat in Haiti: The Diplomatic Correspondence of U.S. Minister
    Frederick Douglass from Haiti, 1889–1891.* Ed. Norma Brown. 1977. 2
    vols.

The Frederick Douglass Papers. Ed. John W. Blassingame et al. 1979– . 4 vols.
    (to date).

The Narrative and Selected Writings. Ed. Michael Meyer. 1984.

W. E. B. Du Bois

1868–1963

WILLIAM EDWARD BURGHARDT DU BOIS was born in the village of Great Barrington, Massachusetts, on February 23, 1868. His father, Alfred, was born in Haiti, and after a stint in the Union army settled in the Berkshires, where he met and married Mary Burghardt, a descendant of a slave brought from West Africa. However, Alfred Du Bois drifted away from the family and never returned to his wife and son. Du Bois's mother, crippled by depression and a stroke, raised her son with the assistance of her brother and sisters.

Du Bois graduated from high school with honors and delivered a speech on the abolition of slavery. However, because of financial difficulties, Du Bois attended Fisk University instead of Harvard, his first choice. Du Bois later took his master's at Harvard, although by then he had shed most of his illusions about the university. He attended classes taught by George Santayana and William James and developed a close relationship with the latter. In 1892, after receiving his degree in history, Du Bois went to the University of Berlin to study. Although he had a deep distrust of orthodox religion, he nevertheless secured a position at the African Methodist Wilberforce College in Xenia, Ohio, and published his dissertation for Harvard, *The Suppression of the African Slave-Trade to the United States of America, 1638–1870* (1896). He then accepted a position to study the black neighborhoods of Philadelphia and compiled the first sociological text on a black American community in the United States: *The Philadelphia Negro* (1899).

At Atlanta University, where he began to teach history and economics in 1897, Du Bois laid the foundations for the field of black sociology. He established annual conferences devoted to "efforts of American Negroes for their own social betterment," and edited its proceedings from 1896 to 1913. He also founded the journals the *Crisis* and, later, *Phylon*. This work, along with his prolific writing, established Du Bois as the leading black literary, educational, and political figure of the early twentieth century.

Du Bois achieved tremendous fame for a collection of essays, *The Souls of Black Folk* (1903), which went through many editions. In 1909 he published a substantial biography of John Brown. His seminal work, *The Negro* (1915), is important in that its theoretical departure was Pan-African: the study of African writing and culture could no longer ignore slavery, as well as the extended links between the peoples of Africa and those of the Caribbean and the Americas. Other important volumes of essays are *Darkwater: Voices from within the Veil* (1920), *The Gift of Black Folk* (1924), *Black Reconstruction* (1935), *Dusk of Dawn* (1940), and many others.

In addition to his nonfiction, Du Bois published several novels over his long literary career. His first was *The Quest of the Silver Fleece* (1911). *Dark Princess* followed in 1928, and after many years Du Bois wrote a trilogy collectively titled *Black Flame*, consisting of *The Ordeal of Mansart* (1957), *Mansart Builds a School* (1959), and *Worlds of Color* (1961).

With the passing of years Du Bois became a problematic leader; his closest disciples found him cold and arrogant and such figures as Claude McKay and Marcus Garvey challenged his achievements and socialist ideology. He was dismissed from the NAACP as its director of special research in 1948; he became a target of domestic anticommunism, being tried in 1951 for being an "unregistered foreign agent" and acquitted by a federal grand jury. In 1961, at the invitation of President Kwame Nkrumah of Ghana, Du Bois traveled to this Western African nation and began to direct the *Encyclopedia Africana* project, joining the U.S. Communist party as well. Denied a U.S. passport because of his political beliefs, Du Bois became a citizen of Ghana and died there on August 27, 1963, at the age of ninety-five. His *Autobiography* was published in 1968, and an edition of his *Complete Published Works* is being compiled by Herbert Aptheker. His wife, Shirley Graham Du Bois, has written a memoir of her life with him, *His Day Is Marching On* (1971).

◈ *Critical Extracts*

W. E. B. DU BOIS   High in the tower, where I sit above the loud complaining of the human sea, I know many souls that toss and whirl and pass, but none there are that intrigue me more than the Souls of White Folk.

Of them I am singularly clairvoyant. I see in and through them. I view them from unusual points of vantage. Not as a foreigner do I come, for I am native, not foreign, bone of their thought and flesh of their language. Mine is not the knowledge of the traveler or the colonial composite of dear memories, words and wonder. Nor yet is my knowledge that which servants have of masters, or mass of class, or capitalist of artisan. Rather I see these souls undressed and from the back and side. I see the working of their entrails. I know their thoughts and they know that I know. This knowledge makes them now embarrassed, now furious! They deny my right to live and be and call me misbirth! My word is to them mere bitterness and my soul, pessimism. And yet as they preach and strut and shout and threaten, crouching as they clutch at rags of facts and fancies to hide their nakedness, they go twisting, flying by my tired eyes and I see them ever stripped,— ugly, human. ⟨. . .⟩

A true and worthy ideal frees and uplifts a people; a false ideal imprisons and lowers. Say to men, earnestly and repeatedly: "Honesty is best, knowledge is power; do unto others as you would be done by." Say this and act it and the nation must move toward it, if not to it. But say to a people: "The one virtue is to be white," and the people rush to the inevitable conclusion, "Kill the 'nigger'!"

Is this not the record of present America? Is not this its headlong progress? Are we not coming more and more, day by day, to making the statement "I am white," the one fundamental tenet of our practical morality? Only when this basic, iron rule is involved is our defense of right nation-wide and prompt. Murder may swagger, theft may rule and prostitution may flourish and the nation gives but spasmodic, intermittent and lukewarm attention. But let the murderer be black or the thief brown or the violator of womanhood have a drop of Negro blood, and the righteousness of indignation sweeps the world. Nor would this fact make the indignation less justifiable did not we all know that it was blackness that was condemned and not crime. ⟨. . .⟩

Here is a civilization that has boasted much. Neither Roman nor Arab, Greek nor Egyptian, Persian nor Mongol ever took himself and his own perfectness with such disconcerting seriousness as the modern white man. We whose shame, humiliation, and deep insult his aggrandizement so often involved were never deceived. We looked at him clearly, with world-old eyes, and saw simply a human being, weak and pitiable and cruel, even as we are and were.

These super-men and world-mastering demi-gods listened, however, to no low tongues of ours, even when we pointed silently to their feet of clay. Perhaps we, as folk of simpler soul and more primitive type, have been most struck in the welter of recent years by the utter failure of white religion.

We have curled our lips in something like contempt as we have witnessed glib apology and weary explanation. Nothing of the sort deceived us. A nation's religion is its life, and as such white Christianity is a miserable failure.

Nor would we be unfair in this criticism: We know that we, too, have failed, as you have, and have rejected many a Buddha, even as you have denied Christ; but we acknowledge our human frailty, while you, claiming super-humanity, scoff endlessly at our shortcomings.

The number of white individuals who are practising with even reasonable approximation the democracy and unselfishness of Jesus Christ is so small and unimportant as to be fit subject for jest in Sunday supplements and in *Punch, Life, Le Rire,* and *Fliegende Blätter.* In her foreign mission work the extraordinary self-deception of white religion is epitomized: solemnly the white world sends five million dollars worth of missionary propaganda to Africa each year and in the same twelve months adds twenty-five million dollars worth of the vilest gin manufactured. Peace to the augurs of Rome!

W. E. B. Du Bois, "The Souls of White Folk," *Darkwater: Voices from Within the Veil* (New York: Harcourt, Brace & Howe, 1920), pp. 29, 34–36

AUGUST MEIER   Of the great trio of Negro leaders, Douglass was the orator, Du Bois the polished writer, and Washington the practical man of affairs. Like Douglass, Du Bois has been known primarily as a protest leader, though he was not as consistent in this role as Douglass. Like Douglass, too, he exhibited a marked oscillation in his ideologies—in fact his was more marked than that of Douglass. Like Douglass he clearly stated the ultimate goals which Washington obscured. Yet Du Bois displayed more of a sense of racial solidarity than Douglass usually did. Nor did he envisage the degree of amalgamation and loss of racial consciousness that Douglass regarded as the *summum bonum.* On the contrary he, like Washington, emphasized race pride and solidarity and economic chauvinism, though after 1905 he no longer championed support of the individualist entrepreneur but favored instead a co-operative economy. Where Washington wanted to make Negroes entrepreneurs and captains of industry in accordance with the American economic dream (a dream shared with less emphasis by Douglass), Du Bois stressed the role of the college-educated elite and later developed a vision of a world largely dominated by the colored races which would combine with the white workers in overthrowing the domination of white capital and thus secure social justice under socialism. All three emphasized the moral values in American culture and the necessity of justice for the Negro if the promise of American life were to be fulfilled. But of the three men it was Douglass who was pre-eminently the moralist, while Washington and Du Bois expressed sharply divergent economic interpretations. Where Douglass and Washington were primarily petit-bourgeois in their outlook, Du Bois played the role of the Marxist intelligentsia. Where the interest of Douglass and Washington in Africa was largely perfunctory, Du Bois exhibited a deep sense of racial identity with Africans. Above all, though only Douglass favored amalgamation, all three had as their goal the integration of Negroes into American society.

Scholar and prophet; mystic and materialist; ardent agitator for political rights and propagandist for economic co-operation; one who espoused an economic interpretation of politics and yet emphasized the necessity of political rights for economic advancement; one who denounced segregation and called for integration into American society in accordance with the principles of human brotherhood and the ideals of democracy, and at the same time one who favored the maintenance of racial solidarity and integrity and a feeling of identity with Negroes elsewhere in the world; an equalitarian who apparently believed in innate racial differences; a Marxist who was fundamentally a middle-class intellectual, Du Bois becomes the epitome of the paradoxes in American Negro thought. In fact, despite his early tendencies toward an accommodating viewpoint, and despite his strong sense of race solidarity and integrity, Du Bois expressed more effectively than any of his contemporaries the protest tendency in Negro thought, and the desire for citizenship rights and integration into American society.

> August Meier, "The Paradox of W. E. B. Du Bois," *Negro Thought in America, 1880–1915: Racial Ideologies in the Age of Booker T. Washington* (Ann Arbor: University of Michigan Press, 1963), pp. 205–6

JOHN OLIVER KILLENS   It was early morning of the March on Washington. We stood in the busy lobby of the Willard Hotel. I believe there were among those with me, chatting quietly, excitedly, nervously, James Baldwin and Sidney Poitier. Outside, Washington, D.C. was like an occupied city, with police and helmeted soldiers everywhere. There were very few civilians on the streets that memorable morning. By air, busses, automobiles, on foot, people were gathering on the outskirts of the city by the tens of thousands. The downtown government district was hushed and awesomely white as only Washington can be. Our group was waiting for transportation to the National Airport, where we were to participate in a press conference before the March began.

Some one walked over to our group and said, "The old man died." Just that. And not one of us asked, "What old man?" We all knew who the old man was, because he was our old man. He belonged to every one of us. And we belonged to him. To some of us he was our patron saint, our teacher and our major prophet. He was Big Daddy? No. He was Big Grand Daddy. More than any other single human being, he, through the sheer power of his vast and profound intelligence, his tireless scholarship and his fierce dedication to the cause of black liberation, had brought us and the other two hundred and fifty thousand souls to this place, to this moment in time and space.

John Oliver Killens, "An Introduction," *The ABC of Color: Selections Chosen by the Author from Over a Half Century of His Writings* by W. E. B. Du Bois (New York: International Publishers, 1969), p. 9

ARNOLD RAMPERSAD   In the years since Du Bois' death in 1963, the memory of his gifts as a poet, scholar, and fighter has stayed alive among the majority of thinking black Americans. For others, though, his contribution has sunk to the status of a footnote in the long history of race relations in the United States. This decline has come in spite of the decades of brilliant political crusading, the beauty and cultural significance of *The Souls of Black Folk*, the power of historical imagination represented by such works as *The Suppression of the African Slave-Trade*, *The Negro*, and *Black Reconstruction in America*, and the innovative and thorough social science of *The Philadelphia Negro*.

But in a way both modest and extraordinary, Du Bois was a maker of history. Although he sometimes raged, he achieved success through his long, slow influence on the thinkers of black America and their white sympathizers and allies. If the history of ideas in Afro-America is ever written, Du Bois should occupy the most conspicuous place. If—even more unlikely—the full history of the impact of blacks on the American mind is ever charted, his education of the whole nation will be seen as significant indeed.

His works have not received the study they deserve, and his modest reputation now rests on grounds that he would not wholly appreciate. He is remembered for his strategy in controversies not always properly understood, and for slogans and concepts that inadequately represent the range of his mind. His words appear to support a variety of contradictory causes and, in common with great bodies of art and literature, are susceptible to such a large number of interpretations that the casual reader is sometimes bewildered.

These inexact views of the man occur because Du Bois' vision was filtered through a variety of experiences possible only in America. He was a product of black and white, poverty and privilege, love and hate. He was of New England and of the South, an alien and an American, a provincial and a cosmopolite, nationalist and communist, Victorian and modern. With the soul of a poet and the intellect of a scientist, he lived at least a double life, continually compelled to respond to the challenge of reconciling opposites. ⟨. . .⟩

His final achievement was in his service to his folk, his nation, and to all those who could comprehend the fuller human significance of the lessons of his life. More than any other individual, he was responsible for the conversion of the facts and episodes of Afro-American history into that coherent, though necessarily diffuse, mythology on which collective self-respect and self-love must inevitably be founded. And far more powerfully than any other American intellectual, he explicated the mysteries of race in a nation which, proud of its racial pluralism, has just begun to show remorse for crimes inspired by racism.

Arnold Rampersad, *The Art and Imagination of W. E. B. Du Bois* (Cambridge, MA: Harvard University Press, 1976), .pp. 291–93

MARION BERGHAHN   It is not unimportant that DuBois's painful experience of the racism in his country came relatively late when his self-confidence had become sufficiently consolidated and could no longer be profoundly shaken. As he himself reports, he experienced hardly any racial problems at school. There were few Afro-Americans in Great Barrington, and it was therefore not necessary to draw a clear line separating blacks from whites, even though such a line existed unofficially. The general contempt for the 'poor, drunken and sloven' Irish and South Germans living in the slums—which the black population shared—helped to obscure the 'color line'. DuBois's schoolmates were often the sons of affluent whites whom he outstripped in intelligence and performance at school and who frequently chose him to be their leader at play. Because of this he thought of himself as belonging to the 'rich and well-to-do', although his own family lived in modest circumstances. ⟨Harold R.⟩ Isaacs thinks that 'his natural impulse was to gravitate to the top'. The older DuBois grew, however, the clearer it became that this 'impulse' was not quite so 'natural'; rather it seems to have originated in a psychological compensating mechanism. For gradually DuBois did grow conscious of the fact that his darker skin and his slightly negroid physiognomy were regarded as a blemish by a number of whites and that 'some human beings even thought it a crime'. But he refused to be disconcerted by this attitude, '. . . although, of course, there were some days of secret tears; rather I was spurred to tireless effort. If they beat me at anything, I was grimly determined to make them sweat for it!' And indeed he succeeded, through diligence and energy, in turning his negroid appearance into an advantage; it set him visibly apart from his peers and helped to emphasise his above-average intelligence all the more clearly. He won the respect of his schoolmates, and this led him to assume that 'the secret of life and the losing of the color bar, then, lay in excellence, in accomplishment . . . There was no real discrimination on account of color—it was all a matter of ability and hard work.' This ethic of work and accomplishment governed his whole life: 'God is Work', one of his fictional characters says. Nor did he ever abandon his childhood belief in the power and superiority of knowledge above all other human activities.

DuBois developed yet another, very characteristic, attitude toward his early youth: in order to avoid being humiliated he never sought contact with whites himself. This meant that his schoolmates were never given an opportunity 'to refuse me invitations; they must seek me out and urge me to come, as indeed they often did. When my presence was not wanted they had only to refrain from asking.' Even when, later, after some initial difficulties, he had won a place at Harvard, he was too proud to seek associations with white students. He even boasted of not having known most of his contemporaries, some of whom became very well known later. Yet he is frank enough to admit that

> something of a certain inferiority complex was possibly a cause
> of this. I was desperately afraid of intruding where I was not wanted;
> . . . I should in fact have been pleased if most of my fellow
> students had wanted to associate with me; if I had been
> popular and envied. But the absence of this made me neither
> unhappy nor morose. I had my 'island within' and it was a
> fair country.

Above all he avoided white or very light-skinned 'black' women and for the same reason rejected any thought of racial mixing: 'I resented the assumption that we desired it.' These and similar statements show how deeply DuBois's pride was hurt by any actual or potential threat of being rejected by the whites. 'He wanted recognition, acceptance, eminence, a life among peers. When he was denied, he cut himself off' (Harold R. Isaacs). Thus DuBois—who had spent his early youth primarily in the company of whites—developed into a passionate black nationalist; it was among blacks that he would find the satisfaction of his pride which the whites had denied him. This need 'to show it to the whites', to prove to them that blacks are equal or even superior to them which grew out of humiliations is one— maybe even the most important—root of his later cultural nationalism, and it explains as well as any other reason his fixation with white culture.

> Marion Berghahn, "Pan-Africa as a Myth in the Literary Work of DuBois," *Images of Africa in Black American Literature* (Totowa, NJ: Rowman & Littlefield, 1977), pp. 69–71

KEITH E. BYERMAN   The first essay in W. E. B. Du Bois's collection, *The Souls of Black Folk* (1903), offers a classic statement of the psychological meaning of being black in America:

> It is a peculiar sensation, this double-consciousness, this sense
> of always looking at one's self through the eyes of others, of measuring
> one's soul by the tape of a world that looks on in amused
> contempt and pity. One ever feels his twoness,—an
> American, a Negro; two souls, two thoughts, two unreconciled
> strivings; two warring ideals in one dark body, whose dogged
> strength alone keeps it from being torn asunder.

The duality described here has been a common theme in black literature from Paul Laurence Dunbar's "We Wear the Mask" (1895) to Toni Morrison's *Song of Solomon* (1977). Du Bois articulated an ambiguity that clearly has significance for black writers, and his book has been recognized for years for its insight. Shortly after publication, Jessie Fauset commended the author of *Souls* as "a man of fine sensibilities" who voiced "the intricacies of the blind maze of thought and action along which the modern, educated colored man or woman struggles." Later commentators have noted the specific image, the veil, that Du Bois used to express the division of the world for blacks and have also identified his basic optimism in arguing that a healing of the split can occur if only his political and moral ideas are accepted.

What has been ignored in all these observations is the fact that Du Bois, in at least two of his essays in the book—"Of the Meaning of Progress" and "Of the Passing of the First-Born"—creates narrators who express a far more ambivalent attitude toward the possibility of ending the war of the two ideals. Though these particular essays are usually seen as autobiographical, careful analysis reveals narrative voices that are very different from the rational, morally confident Du Bois of the more expository chapters. These uncertain speakers, in the process of presenting their stories, show us rather than tell us the deep psychological implication of living the life of double-consciousness. The implicit suggestion is that the reformist arguments of most of *Souls* do not deal with the deeper consequences of racism. The author who juxtaposes such arguments with unresolved psychological dramas is clearly a man who is himself of two minds about the nature of racism and the possibilities for its eradication. He argues for a rational approach, but his subtler efforts, as in the creation of narrators, indicate a recognition that the psychological and moral effects of the problem raise serious doubts about his reform proposals. Significantly, he does not attempt to resolve this conflict of optimism and pessimism; instead he explores its dramatic possibilities. By analyzing the narrators through which he presents this drama, it becomes possible to see the greater literary significance and moral complexity of a work that is a major contribution to black literature specifically but also to American literature in general. ⟨. . .⟩

"Of the Meaning of Progress" and "Of the Passing of the First-Born" are generally taken as the autobiographical essays in a work that uses many different disciplines and forms to communicate its egalitarian ideology. The "facts" of the essays certainly correspond to the facts of Du Bois's life. But more important than those facts are the means by which they are expressed. Du Bois creates narrative characters who reveal themselves as far more complex than the narrative facts would lead us to believe. They show us, in the process of telling their tales, the deeper and more serious impact that racism has on even those blacks who are relatively sophisticated and successful. They are figures who have had their idealism destroyed and, in the case of the father, their instincts distorted. Though they both are carrying on their lives at the end of their stories, they no longer have vitality or certainty.

The success of such creations suggests that the real literary achievement of *The Souls of Black Folk* is not in the genteel and often archaic nature of its language, nor in the fortuitous selection of the image of the veil, nor even in the rhetorical power of its combination of a significant theme with a range of classical literary devices. Instead, its achievement can be found in Du Bois's ability to dramatize the meaning of being black in America. It is in effectively showing as well as telling that he communicates the deeper significance of racism. He shows the impact of prejudices on the black mind and clearly understands that this impact will not be removed by his reform proposals. At its most insidious, racism destroys both the meaning of life and the desire to live. Du Bois's recognition of such a dark reality and his creation of narrators to express it make *The Souls of Black Folk* a major literary achievement.

Keith E. Byerman, "Hearts of Darkness: Narrative Voices in *The Souls of Black Folk*," *American Literary Realism* 14, No. 1 (Spring 1981): 43–44, 50–51

JANE CAMPBELL   As the only romancer of post-Reconstruction to lay bare the plight of lower-class blacks, Du Bois ⟨in *The Quest of the Silver Fleece*⟩ reveals the sharecropping system to be very little different from slavery. The Christmas season illustrates the system's duplicity. Colonel Creswell, one of "the lords of the soil," converses with his clerks about the proper way to distribute the wages to one sharecropper: "Well, he's a good nigger and needs encouragement; cancel his debt and give him ten dollars for Christmas." Creswell perceives that another farmer, having raised a bountiful crop, is trying to move away from the plantation. To ensure his servitude, Creswell advises, "Keep him in debt, but let him draw what he wants." Similarly, when Zora and Bles, the romance's protagonists, raise a good crop, Harry Creswell cheats Zora out of her money and leaves her twenty-five dollars in debt. Through these and other scenes, Du Bois fictionalizes the manipulation of the sharecroppers that takes place in part because the landlords are dishonest, in part because the workers themselves are too ignorant to understand the system and too acculturated to question it. Only through the "talented tenth's" messianic power that Du Bois celebrates in *The Souls of Black Folk* (1903) can the uneducated be saved from such exploitation. Therefore, when Bles and Zora return from Washington, they organize the people to fight against the sharecropping system.

In contrast, the political corruption that Bles and Zora confront in Washington appears indomitable. Du Bois goes further than Griggs and Chesnutt in depicting the horror and complexity of post-Reconstruction politics. His distance from his material is such that he achieves an almost naturalistic work; unlike Griggs and Chesnutt he rarely editorializes but simply presents scenes and characters responsible for the corruption. On a quest for wealth, power, and status, all are enmeshed in a web of intrigue and backstabbing that coolly dispenses with those incapable of playing by the rules. Caroline Wynn, an educated mulatta, has become a senator's mistress to further her own interests. Eager to marry a politician, she suggests to the senator that Bles, her suitor, be given an office. Mrs. Vanderpool, a wealthy and influential woman, agrees to promote Bles for treasurer, in hopes of securing the French ambassadorship for her husband. When Bles speaks against the Republican party for refusing to support an education bill, however, the position of treasurer goes to Sam Stillings, a former friend of Bles. Seeing her chance, Caroline jilts Bles to marry Sam. Further complicating the unbelievable tangle of coincidence, Mary Taylor Creswell, whose husband Harry has been suggested for the French ambassadorship instead of the dissolute Vanderpool, is in turn framed by Mrs. Vanderpool for having deliberately given a prize to a sculpture submitted by Caroline. When the press discovers that the prize has gone to a black, Creswell loses the appointment.

In all these machinations, Du Bois reveals that he, like Chesnutt, sees historical process as resulting from human needs for security, wealth, and status and from humanity's ability to learn the methods to satisfy those needs. ⟨Herbert⟩ Aptheker delineates the positive aspect of this view of history when he summarizes Du Bois's essay "Mr. Sorokin's Systems." "The historian," Du Bois held, ". . . must believe that creative human initiative, working outside mechanical sequence, directs and changes the course of human action and so history . . . it is man who causes movement and change." And for Du Bois, as for Griggs and Chesnutt, education represents the primary means for the individual to effect change. But the type of education acquired is of great significance. To analyze the educational situation for black America during post-Reconstruction one must acknowledge Booker T. Washington. Chesnutt and Washington were good friends. Although Chesnutt disagreed with Washington's insistence on industrial education, their friendship prevented Chesnutt in his published writings from disparaging Washington's ideas. Both Chesnutt and Griggs reacted to Washington's rejection of higher educational aims, his elevation of industrial work, but neither openly denounced him as did Du Bois. In "Of Mr. Booker T. Washington and Others," Du Bois enunciates his view that not only had Washington's educational and political theories sped disenfranchisement and withdrawal of aid to black colleges, but these same blacks could not survive without the voting privileges Washington discounted. Furthermore, Washington's insistence on self-respect conflicted with his insistence on silent submission. Finally, though Washington deprecated black colleges and supported common-schools, neither his own Tuskegee Institute nor the common-schools could stay open without teachers, who had to attend black colleges. Du Bois thus exposes the fundamental contradictions of Washington's thought. Accordingly, he organized the Niagara Movement in 1905 to fight discrimination, segregation, and Washington's accommodationist policies.

Jane Campbell, "Visions of Transcendence in W. E. B. Du Bois's *The Quest of the Silver Fleece* and William Attaway's *Blood on the Forge*," *Mythic Black Fiction: The Transformation of History* (Knoxville: University of Tennessee Press, 1986), pp. 66–68

NELLIE Y. McKAY ⟨. . .⟩ while it is true that Du Bois's autobiographies are about "ideas" and do not represent the archetypal "journey" of the man, the extent to which he includes the influences of women's experience, and especially those of black women, on his thinking; his recognition of gender oppression; and his acceptance of the worth of his emotional and spiritual feelings makes his work distinctive. More than any other black man in our history, his three autobiographies demonstrate that black women have been central to the development of his intellectual thought. In his old age he would say that he had always had more friends among black women than among black men; that he was less attracted to relationships with the men of the race because many of them "imitated an American culture which [he] did not share." Using the criteria of inclusiveness of experience, and an awareness of race and gender oppression as aspects of the composition of feminist autobiography, Du Bois comes closer to consciously repudiating the intellectual/emotional, mind/body split than many other writers of intellectual autobiography.

To begin at the beginning, we know that Du Bois had a perception that black folk have "souls" that not only understand the problems of the Veil, but also embody peculiarly transcending sensibilities that enhance their humanity. We also know that he was aware that the folk were not all men. If anything can be said about his views on the souls of black women folk, it is that he felt that they had struggled through to an even higher plane than black men had. He was not afraid to acknowledge his own spiritual-emotional feelings, and he was not afraid to acknowledge their manifestations in the lives of others, including women. In like manner, he was not afraid to recognize the more concrete elements of human experience. It is this kind of inclusive perspective on experience that makes his autobiographies stand out for me. ⟨. . .⟩

There is little doubt that the souls of black women folk were close to Du Bois's consciousness throughout his life—that is, that the importance of women, beyond their socially defined roles of subordination to men, was a matter that he took very seriously.

Nellie Y. McKay, "The Souls of Black Women Folk in the Writings of W. E. B. Du Bois," *Reading Black, Reading Feminist: A Critical Anthology*, ed. Henry Louis Gates, Jr. (New York: Meridian, 1990), pp. 227–28

RICHARD KOSTELANETZ   In the end, although Du Bois's novels were published over a span of fifty years, their attitudes on politics are nearly all of a single piece. In *The Quest of the Silver Fleece*, the possibilities of individual African-American independence within the South are tested and found wanting; yet opportunities in the North are hardly better. Among the politically favorable portraits are, first, the few kindly whites who teach Southern blacks and, second, the agitators for a well-organized communal settlement that would only compete with the white South. In *Dark Princess*, not only the South but also the North is rejected, as the novel's protagonist expatriates to India; and the novel predicts that all colored people will claim as their own the land they now occupy. In the *Black Flame* trilogy, nearly all Afro-American possibilities in America are tested and, finally, rejected; and again expatriation, particularly to Africa, is favored, in addition to alliances with international Communism. Du Bois's novels, in addition to posing general questions, also define a range of options that Richard Wright and Ralph Ellison, political novelists both, subsequently incorporated into their own fictions.

> Richard Kostelanetz, "W. E. B. Du Bois," *Politics in the African-American Novel* (Westport, CT: Greenwood Press, 1991), p. 66

Bibliography

The Suppression of the African Slave-Trade to the United States of America, 1638–1870. 1896.

Mortality among Negroes in Cities (editor). 1896.

Social and Physical Condition of Negroes in Cities (editor). 1897.

The Conservation of Races. 1897.

Some Efforts of American Negroes for Their Own Social Betterment (editor). 1898.

Careers Open to Young Negro-Americans. 1898.

The College-Bred Negro. c. 1898.

The Negro in Business (editor). 1899.

The Philadelphia Negro (with Isabel Eaton). 1899.

Memorial to the Legislature of Georgia on the Hardwick Bill (with others). 1899.

The College-Bred Negro (editor). 1900.

The Negro Common School (editor). 1901.

Results of Ten Tuskegee Negro Conferences. 1901.

A Select Bibliography of the American Negro. 1901.

The Negro Artisan (editor). 1902.

The Negro Church (editor). 1903.

Some Notes on the Negroes in New York City. 1903.

The Souls of Black Folk: Essays and Sketches. 1903.

A Bibliography of Negro Folk Songs. 1903.

Heredity and the Public Schools: A Lecture Delivered under the Auspices of the Principals' Association of the Colored Schools of Washington. 1904.

Some Notes on Negro Crime, Particularly in Georgia (editor). 1904.

A Select Bibliography of the Negro American (editor). 1905.
Niagara Movement—Declaration of Principles (with others). 1905.
The Health and Physique of the Negro American (editor). 1906.
Economic Co-operation among Negro Americans (editor). 1907.
The Negro American Family (editor). 1908.
Efforts for Social Betterment among Negro Americans (editor). 1909.
John Brown. 1909.
The College-Bred Negro American (editor; with Augustus Granville Dill). 1910.
College-Bred Negro Communities: Address at Brookline, Massachusetts. 1910.
Race Relations in the United States: An Appeal to England (with others). 1910.
The Common School and the Negro American (editor; with Augustus Granville
        Dill). 1911.
The Quest of the Silver Fleece. 1911.
The Social Evolution of the Black South. 1911.
The Negro American Artisan (editor; with Augustus Granville Dill). 1912.
Disenfranchisement. 1912.
Morals and Manners among Negro Americans (editor; with Augustus Granville
        Dill). 1914.
A Half Century of Freedom. 1914.
The Negro. 1915.
Darkwater: Voices from within the Veil. 1920.
The Gift of Black Folk: The Negroes in the Making of America. 1924.
The Amenia Conference: An Historic Negro Gathering. 1925.
Dark Princess: A Romance. 1928.
Notes on the Negro in City Politics. 1929.
Africa—Its Place in Modern History. 1930.
Africa: Its Geography, People and Products. 1930.
A Study of the Atlanta University Federal Housing Area. 1934.
*Black Reconstruction: An Essay toward a History of the Part Which Black Folk
        Played in the Attempt to Reconstruct Democracy in America, 1860–1880.*
        1935.
What the Negro Has Done for the United States and Texas. 1936.
Race Philosophy and Policies for Negro Life in the North. 1936.
*A Pageant in Seven Decades, 1868–1938: An Address Delivered on the Occasion
        of His Seventieth Birthday at the University Convocation of Atlanta Univer-
        sity, Morehouse College, and Spelman College.* 1938.
*Black Folk, Then and Now: An Essay in the History and Sociology of the Negro
        Race.* 1939.
Dusk of Dawn: An Essay toward an Autobiography of a Race Concept. 1940.
*Conference of Negro Land Grant Colleges for Coordinating a Program of Coopera-
        tive Social Studies* (editor). 1943.

Conference of Negro Land Grant Colleges for Coordinating a Program of Cooperative Social Studies (editor). 1944.

Color and Democracy: Colonies and Peace. 1945.

Encyclopedia of the Negro (with others). 1945, 1946.

Human Rights for All Minorities. 1945.

The World and Africa: An Inquiry into the Part Which Africa Has Played in World History. 1947.

An Appeal to the World (editor). 1947.

Peace Is Dangerous. 1951.

In Battle for Peace: The Story of My 83rd Birthday. 1952.

What Is Wrong with the United States. 1954.

The Story of Benjamin Franklin. 1956.

The Ordeal of Mansart. 1957.

Mansart Builds a School. 1959.

Socialism Today. 1959.

Africa in Battle against Colonialism, Racialism, Imperialism. 1960.

Worlds of Color. 1961.

An ABC of Color: Selections from Over a Half Century of the Writings of W. E. B. Du Bois. 1963, 1969.

The Autobiography of W. E. B. Du Bois: A Soliloquy on Viewing My Life from the Last Decade of Its First Century. 1968.

W. E. B. Du Bois: A Reader. Ed. Meyer Weinberg. 1970.

W. E. B. Du Bois Speaks: Speeches and Addresses. Ed. Philip S. Foner. 1970. 2 vols.

A W. E. B. Du Bois Reader. Ed. Andrew G. Paschal. 1971.

The Seventh Son: The Thought and Writings of W. E. B. Du Bois. Ed. Julius Lester. 1971.

The Crisis Writings. Ed. Daniel Walden. 1972.

The Education of Black People: Ten Critiques, 1906–1960. Ed. Herbert Aptheker. 1973.

Du Bois on the Importance of Africa in World History. 1978.

Complete Published Works. Ed. Herbert Aptheker. 1980– .

Against Racism: Unpublished Essays, Papers, Addresses, 1887–1961. Ed. Herbert Aptheker. 1985.

Writings. 1986.

W. E. B. Du Bois on Sociology and the Black Community. Ed. Dan S. Green and Edwin D. Driver. 1987.

The Atlanta Conference. n.d.

The Damnation of Women. n.d.

The Immortal Child: Background on Crises in Education. n.d.

Paul Laurence Dunbar
1872–1906

PAUL LAURENCE DUNBAR was born in Dayton, Ohio, on June 27, 1872, the son of former slaves. He attended a local high school where he was the only black enrolled and was the editor of the school paper. After school Dunbar worked as an elevator boy in Dayton but also began to contribute poems and stories to local newspapers. He met Charles Thatcher, a lawyer from Toledo who gave him substantial support in launching his literary career. Dunbar also worked as a clerk in the Haitian Pavilion at the World's Columbian Exposition in Chicago, where he met Frederick Douglass and other black notables.

Dunbar published poems in Dayton newspapers and brought out two verse collections, *Oak and Ivy* and *Majors and Minors*, privately printed in 1893 and 1895, respectively. William Dean Howells's influential review of the latter in *Harper's Weekly* marked the beginning of Dunbar's fame as a poet on a national level. Howells also wrote the introduction to Dunbar's next collection, *Lyrics of Lowly Life* (1896), which was well received. In 1897 Dunbar ventured to England for public readings and met and collaborated with composer Samuel Coleridge-Taylor. Later that year he became employed as reading room assistant in the Library of Congress in Washington, D.C.

In 1898 Dunbar married Alice Ruth Moore, a writer. In that same year he published his first novel, *The Uncalled*, followed by three others in rapid succession: *The Love of Landry* (1900), *The Fanatics* (1901), and *The Sport of the Gods* (1902). In 1899 he participated with Booker T. Washington and W. E. B. Du Bois in readings to raise funds for the Tuskegee Institute, a southern college for black American students; the following year he took part in Du Bois's conferences on black American issues at Atlanta University. Dunbar also retained a fondness for the Republican party, and in particular Theodore Roosevelt; he participated in this president's inaugural parades, and in 1905 he wrote a poem for the candidate's campaign.

Dunbar's health began to fail around 1900 and he died of tuberculosis on February 8, 1906. His *Complete Poems* was published in 1913. Dunbar was most admired in his own time, and is best remembered today, for his poems and stories written in black dialect. He was the first black author to employ this device, and was inspired, in part, by the example of Robert Burns.

◈ *Critical Extracts*

BENJAMIN BRAWLEY   Dunbar's conception of his art was based on his theory of life. He felt that he was first of all a man, then an American, and incidentally a Negro. To a world that looked upon him primarily as a Negro and wanted to hear from him simply in his capacity as a Negro, he was thus a little difficult to understand. He never regarded the dialect poems as his best work, and, as he said in the eight lines entitled "The Poet," when one tried to sing of the greatest themes in life, it was hard to have the world praise only "a jingle in a broken tongue." His position was debatable, of course, but that was the way he felt. At the meeting at the Waldorf-Astoria a reporter asked about the quality of the poetry written by Negroes as compared with that of white people. Dunbar replied, "The predominating power of the African race is lyric. In that I should expect the writers of my race to excel. But, broadly speaking, their poetry will not be exotic or differ much from that of the whites. . . . For two hundred and fifty years the environment of the Negro has been American, in every respect the same as that of all other Americans." "But isn't there," continued the interviewer, "a certain tropic warmth, a cast of temperament that belongs of right to the African race?" "Ah," said the poet, "what you speak of is going to be a loss. It is inevitable. We must write like the white men. I do not mean imitate them; but our life is now the same." Then he added: "I hope you are not one of those who would hold the Negro down to a certain kind of poetry—dialect and concerning only scenes on plantations in the South?"

To a later school of Negro writers, one more definitely conscious of race, Dunbar thus appears as somewhat artificial. The difference is that wrought by the World War. About the close of that conflict Marcus Garvey, by a positively radical program, made black a fashionable color. It was something not to be apologized for, but exploited. Thenceforth one heard much about "the new Negro," and for a while Harlem was a literary capital. In Dunbar's time, however, black was not fashionable. The burden still rested upon the Negro to prove that he could do what any other man could do, and in America that meant to use the white man's technique and meet the white man's standard of excellence. It was to this task that Dunbar addressed himself. This was the test that he felt he had to satisfy, and not many will doubt that he met it admirably.

Benjamin Brawley, *Paul Laurence Dunbar: Poet of His People* (Chapel Hill: University of North Carolina Press, 1936), pp. 76–77

THEODORA W. DANIEL   Dunbar's prose stories were yet another channel through which he called attention to the failings of American democracy as applied to his race. His resentment of the old, old custom of assigning a "place" to the Negro beyond which he should not advance, ability and initiative notwithstanding, is evident in "The Scapegoat." The scapegoat is a Negro political boss who is sacrificed upon the altar of political reform by his party. Old Judge Davis, a prominent party man, is spokesman for his kind of racial bigot everywhere and for all time.

"Asbury," he said, "you are—you are—well, you ought to be white, that's all. When we find a black man like you we send him to State's prison. If you were white, you'd go to the Senate."

According to democratic theory, the accused is presumed to be innocent until guilt is definitely established. All too often, however, when a Negro is suspect the principle is reversed and guilt is automatically assumed. The violation of this tenet of democracy is subjected to a subtle but searching criticism in "The Lynching of Jube Benson." Here the narrator, Dr. Melville, entertains a group of friends with the revolting details of a lynching which followed the murder of his fiancée. As the innocent black man-of-all-work gasped his last, the real murderer is discovered—a white man with a blackened face. The doctor, who had always loved old Jube and been convinced of the old Negro's love for him and "Miss Annie," thus accounts for his readiness to believe Jube guilty:

"A false education, I reckon, one false from the beginning. I saw his black face glooming there in the half light and I could only think of him as a monster. It's tradition. At first I was told that the black man would catch me, and when I got over that, they taught me that the devil was black, and when I had recovered from the sickness of that belief, here was Jube and his fellows with faces of menacing blackness. There was only one conclusion: This black man stood for all the powers of evil, the result of whose machinations had been gathering in my mind from childhood up. . . ."

Theodora W. Daniel, "Paul Laurence Dunbar and the Democratic Ideal," *Negro History Bulletin* 6, No. 9 (June 1943): 207–8

DARWIN TURNER   Even if Dunbar had been completely free to write scathing protest about the South, he could not have written it, or would have written it ineptly. His experiences and those of his family had not compelled him to hate white people as a group or the South as a region. After Dunbar was twenty, every major job he secured, every publication, and all national recognition resulted directly from the assistance of white benefactors. It is not remarkable that Dunbar assumed that successful Negroes need such help or that, knowing the actuality of Northern benefactors, he believed in the existence of their Southern counterparts. Dunbar was not a unique disciple of such a creed. In *The Ordeal of Mansart*, the militant W. E. B. DuBois has described the manner in which intelligent freedmen sought salvation with the assistance of Southern aristocrats.

As his personal experiences freed him from bitterness towards Caucasians as a group, so his family's experiences relieved bitterness towards the South. The experiences of his parents in slavery probably had been milder than most. His father had been trained in a trade and had been taught to read, write, and compute. As a semi-skilled worker occasionally hired out, he fared better than the average field hand. Irony rather than bitterness is the dominant tone in "The Ingrate," a story Dunbar based on his father's life. Although Dunbar's mother had experienced unpleasantness (as what slave did not), her life as a house slave in Kentucky undoubtedly was easier than that of a slave in the deeper South.

Even had his experiences prompted protest against the South, his social and economic philosophies would have militated against it. Believing that America would prosper only if all citizens recognized their interdependence, he sought to win respect for Negroes by showing that, instead of sulking about the past, they were ready to participate in the joint effort to create a new America. In the poems of *Majors and Minors* (1895) and the stories of *Folks from Dixie* (1898), he repeatedly emphasized the ability and willingness of Negroes to forgive white Americans for previous injustices.

Dunbar's noble sentiments and protagonists reveal not only a naive political philosophy but also a romantic and idealized concept of society. He believed in right rule by an aristocracy based on birth and blood which assured culture, good breeding, and all the virtues appropriate to a gentleman.

He further believed that Negroes, instead of condemning such a society, must prove themselves worthy of a place in it by showing that they had civilized themselves to a level above the savagery which he assumed to be characteristic of Africa. Furthermore, having been reared in Dayton, Ohio, he distrusted big cities and industrialization. Provincially, he assumed the good life for the uneducated to be the life of a farmer in a small western or mid-western settlement or the life of a sharecropper for a benevolent Southern aristocrat. Neither a scholar, political scientist, nor economist, he naively offered an agrarian myth as a shield against the painful reality of discrimination in cities. ⟨. . .⟩

In summary, Dunbar's experiences, his social and economic philosophies, and his artistic ideals limited his criticism of the South. This fact, however, should not imply, as some suppose, that Dunbar accepted the total myth of the plantation tradition. In reality, he was no more willing to assume the romanticized plantation to be characteristic of the entire South than he was willing to deny that some slaves had loved their masters or had behaved foolishly.

Darwin Turner, "Paul Laurence Dunbar: The Rejected Symbol," *Journal of Negro History* 52, No. 1 (January 1967): 2–4

CHARLES R. LARSON   That the protest is missing from much of his earlier writing there can be little doubt. It will be the premise of this article, however, to illustrate that in his novels, at least, Dunbar was becoming more and more concerned with racial issues during the course of his brief, five-year novelistic career; and, further, as illustrated in his four novels, that this social concern coupled with a slow but increasing move in the direction of literary naturalism is clearly apparent by the time of Dunbar's early death. Had he lived another ten or fifteen years—or even five—had he not died at thirty-four, there are indications that the term *Uncle Tom* might never have been applied to his writing. ⟨. . .⟩

In his biography of Dunbar, Brawley has said, "Dunbar's conception of his art was based on his theory of life. He felt that he was first of all a man, then an American, and incidentally a Negro." It is in this quotation, I believe, that the key to Dunbar's novelistic achievement may be seen. It seems unfair to criticize him for being an Uncle Tom simply because he was writing primarily for a white audience. In no way could he have been a financial success had he written solely for the Negro reading audience of his day. Neither does it seem fair to criticize his early novels because they fail to take a conscious stand against the social atrocities leveled on the

Negro race. The protest is there, be it latent and somewhat hidden, even in the first two novels. The remaining two take a much more direct stand against the problems which were undoubtedly eating at Dunbar's conscience throughout his entire lifetime. From these last two novels, it seems almost certain that had Paul Laurence Dunbar lived a few more years, his protest would probably have been vitriolic enough to eradicate all the derogatory terms which have since been leveled against his work.

Charles R. Larson, "The Novels of Paul Laurence Dunbar," *Phylon* 29, No. 3 (Fall 1968): 257, 270–71

ADDISON GAYLE, JR.   As he looked forward to the spring and the trip back East, he worked diligently on the novel, *The Love of Landry*. The editor had asked for "a light novel," and this book filled the bill. It was a love story and took place in Colorado. Mildred, the heroine, comes West to regain her health. There she meets and falls in love with a cowboy named Landry. However, the affair is opposed by one of Mildred's relatives, Aunt Annesley, who lives in the East. During a cattle stampede, the heroine is saved by Landry. For this act, he wins her hand. She is cured and finds both happiness and health.

Once again, despite such a slight plot, Dunbar manages to impose his personal experiences on the novel. Each of the major characters represents some aspect of Dunbar's experiences: Arthur Heathclift, the English suitor for the hand of the heroine, a man who "smells of civilization," is a character modeled after Englishmen whom the poet had met during his stay in England. Heathclift is, to be sure, a poor stereotype of an Englishman, yet he represents Dunbar's idea of a civilized man. John Osborne is the kind, considerate father. He reminds one of the equally kind and considerate Doctor Tobey. Dunbar cherished Tobey's friendship as small boys cherish their relationship with their fathers. There is Aunt Annesley who attempts to interfere in the romance between Landry and Mildred, just as Alice's parents had attempted to interfere with their romance. Mildred, the heroine, suffers from tuberculosis. Like Dunbar, she is forced to come to Colorado to regain her health. Landry Thaler whose name, Landry, reminds one of land, is a man of the earth. Once a part of the frustration and chaos of the city, he has forsaken urban America and come back to nature. With such characters—each symbolizing different aspects of his character—Dunbar wrote a novel in which he, once again, deals with the theme of personal freedom.

Like the characters in his first novel, *The Uncalled*, the characters in his second novel are also white. However, where Freddie Brent, the hero of

The Uncalled, sought freedom from the iron grip of Hester Prime, Mildred and Landry, heroine and hero of *The Love of Landry,* seek freedom from the civilized world. The novel depicts a conflict between the civilized world and the world of nature: "Nothing," the author states in the novel, "is quite so conceited as what we call civilization. And what does it mean after all except to lie gracefully, to cheat legally and to live as far away from God and nature as the world limit will allow." ⟨. . .⟩

Anticipating death—perhaps even with an unconscious wish for it—is there any reason to be surprised that he should imagine himself to be the healthy, physically vibrant, psychologically free Landry Thaler? When Landry throws himself into the midst of thousands of enraged cattle, he throws himself into the face of death with reckless abandon. Since he has mastered the world, it no longer threatens him. Only death threatens him, and Landry takes on this dreaded foe and wins. Dunbar did not believe that he could win. However, like Landry, he had ceased to be afraid of what the long night of "easeful sleep" might mean; he had ceased to be awed by the mystery of it all. The peace that he sought in life, the freedom, came only when he created out of a sense of reality as he knew it, when he created in his white characters images of himself. *The Love of Landry* is a poor novel. But as the account of a poetic spirit seeking escape, seeking release from the bars and cages of life, of a dying soul attempting to lessen the impact of pain upon the still living, it is a remarkable accomplishment.

Addison Gayle, Jr., *Oak and Ivy: A Biography of Paul Laurence Dunbar* (Garden City, NY: Doubleday, 1971), pp. 120–21, 124–25

ROBERT BONE   Throughout Dunbar's fiction, the Northern city is depicted as a repository of false ideals. Anti-heroes, or negative exemplars, are created to embody these false values and illusory goals. Typically they are youthful migrants who succumb to the temptations of gambling, drinking, street crime, disease, or promiscuity. "Silas Jackson" is the purest story of its kind. It deals with a Virginia farmboy who becomes a waiter at a resort hotel. Eventually he is corrupted and destroyed by an opportunity to join a troupe of Negro singers in New York. Like Silas Bollender, he returns from his excursion in disgrace: ". . . spent, broken, hopeless, all contentment and simplicity gone, he turned his face toward his native fields."

A variation on the theme of false ambition is what might be called the carpetbagger theme. Here the protagonist is tempted by a get-rich-quick scheme which promises to bring success without the trouble of hard work. Such a scheme might involve political patronage ("Mr. Cornelius Johnson,

Office Seeker"), real estate manipulation ("The Promoter"), or the policy game ("The Trustfulness of Polly"), but always the protagonist falls victim to his own avarice. In the end his Eldorado vanishes, and he is brought low. The moral of these tales is Washingtonian: only through hard work and sacrifice can the black man hope to improve his lot.

Some of Dunbar's overly ambitious blacks are undone by their own pretentiousness and pride. These are the boastful ones, who insist on flaunting their prosperity. Success turns their heads; they put on airs, become pompous, and adopt a condescending attitude toward their less fortunate brothers. In imitation of the white aristocracy they buy expensive clothes, assume fancy names, cultivate impressive manners, and in short become dandified. Such stories as "The Wisdom of Silence," "Johnsonham, Jr." and "The Home-Coming of 'Rastus Smith" warn the blacks to keep a low profile and do nothing to arouse the envy of their enemies.

> Robert Bone, *Down Home: A History of Afro-American Short Fiction from Its Beginnings to the End of the Harlem Renaissance* (New York: G. P. Putnam's Sons, 1975), p. 65

KENNY J. WILLIAMS   Those who condemn him for his lack of involvement must permit him the right to select his personal view of the role of the writer. His literary creed was certainly an expedient one for the closing years of the nineteenth century. Yet, through his sometimes "race-less" novels Dunbar was able to demonstrate implicitly—although he too was not the most skillful craftsman—that there are some human values which transcend race. For example, in his first novel, *The Uncalled*, the relationship between Freddie Brent and his guardian is a basic relationship and illustrates the conflicts which frequently arise when one person of an older generation attempts to superimpose his will upon one of the younger generation. The novel also demonstrates Dunbar's negative attitude toward the city, an attitude which he was to express time and time again and which was fully explored in his last novel, *The Sport of the Gods*. Romanticist that he was, he dealt with the small-town environment and looked at the city— as had other romantics—as a place of potential evil and degradation for the individual. But as he viewed the conflict between the agrarian values of American life and the rising interest in the city, Dunbar's novels evince a growing awareness not only of the realistic method but also of the hypocrisy of American society. Thus one can see even before *The Sport of the Gods* that Dunbar did indeed deal with social issues and with the racial struggles of this nation.

Interestingly enough, Dunbar frequently relied rather heavily upon his own experiences for his novels. In *The Uncalled* he expanded his own interest in the ministry in order to tell the story of a youngster adopted by a prudish woman of a small-town community and then literally forced by her into the ministry. While decidedly not the great American novel, it does present some realistic conflicts between characters in addition to being a sentimental story in the nineteenth-century tradition. In *The Love of Landry* his search for health in Colorado became the basis for the story of Mildred Osborne, who also goes to Colorado to seek health and who becomes greater by virtue of her association with nature. Commenting on the purpose for Mildred's trip, Dunbar muses rather pathetically in the novel:

> With all the faith one may have in one's self, with all the strong
> hopefulness of youth, it is yet a terrible thing to be forced
> away from home, from all one loves, to an unknown, uncared-
> for country, there to fight, hand to hand with death, an
> uncertain fight. There is none of the rush and clamour of battle
> that keeps up the soldier's courage. There is no clang of the
> instruments of war. The panting warrior hears no loud huzzas,
> and yet the deadly combat goes on; in the still night, when
> all the world's asleep, in the gray day, in the pale morning, it
> goes on, and no one knows it save himself and death. Then
> if he goes down, he knows no hero's honors; if he wins, he has
> no special praise. And yet, it is a terrible, lone, still fight.
> Kenny J. Williams, "The Masking of the Novelist," *A Singer in the Dawn: Reinterpretations of Paul Laurence Dunbar*, ed. Jay Martin (New York: Dodd, Mead, 1975), pp. 168–69

HOUSTON A. BAKER, JR.   The title ⟨of *The Sport of the Gods*⟩ finds its meaning, not in the historically documented betrayals and confusions of American Reconstructions, but in the domain of literature. The blinded and deceived Gloucester of Shakespeare's drama *King Lear* remarks: "As flies to wanton boys are we to the Gods; / They kill us for their sport." The origin and nature of the world, this utterance implies, are functions of capricious supernaturals. The mythic universe of discourse is thus invoked in explanation of man's failings: Man is nothing special. He is a toy in the ludic world of the gods. While the title alone suggests *The Sport of the Gods'* association with Gloucester's mythic view of human events, the concluding line of the novel's narrator suggests an even more direct parallel. The novel ends as follows: "It was not a happy life [that of the black servant Berry Hamilton and his wife, who have returned to the South], but it was all that was left to them, and they took it up without complaint for they knew they were powerless against some Will infinitely stronger than their own." An apotheosized Will "infinitely stronger" than human powers can only exist in a world of myth.

The "limitless" freedom of myth and its efficacy as a causal explanation in human affairs, however, exist in the works of both the Renaissance dramatist and the Afro-American novelist as ironic postulates. There may well be powerful, invisible beings in the wings, but the reader of *King Lear* is aware that the play's sufferings and deaths have more to do with distinctively human shortcomings than with the ludic wielding of authority by immortals. That Gloucester, whose incredible folly is matched only by that of his aged counterpart Lear, is the character who offers "the sport of the Gods" as explanation reinforces a reader's decision to concentrate on human agents and actions in understanding Shakespeare's drama. Similarly, having followed the controlling voice of the narrator from the first to the concluding line of *The Sport of the Gods*, a reader knows there is little need to summon incomprehensible supernatural powers to explain the human affairs represented in the novel.

The characters of Dunbar's work are, finally, victims of their own individual modes of processing reality. Their failings are paradoxical results of their peculiarly human ability (and inclination) to form theories of knowledge, to construct what Walter Pater calls in *The Renaissance* "habits of thought." The narrator's recourse to what seems a mythic dimension (an invincible "Will"), therefore, like Gloucester's evocation of the Gods in *Lear*, not only stands in ironic contrast to the novel's representations of a mundane reality but also suggests ⟨. . .⟩ an authorial awareness on Dunbar's part crucial to a full, blues understanding of his narrative. ⟨. . .⟩

The Sport of the Gods ⟨. . .⟩ is Dunbar's symbolic "acting out" of the effects of American life and letters of a supreme, revelatory fiction that will enable human beings to see life steadily and whole, enabling them to break free from both their "artistic" and "ordinary" modes of structuring experience. The novel thus captures in subtly energetic ways a dream of American form. It specifically explores the proposition that a literary tradition governed by plantation and coon-show images of Afro-Americans can be altered through an ironic, symbolic, fictive (blues) manipulation of such images and the tradition of which they are a formative part.

The Plantation Tradition and its images (like the coon show) did not spring, ab nihilo, from Dunbar's mind. Both were intrinsic to the world of artistic discourse institutionalized in the society of his era. Hence, while he was at liberty to suggest in *The Sport of the Gods* a radical alteration of the prevailing universe of fictive discourse, Dunbar was at the same time hedged round by the conventions—the social existence, as it were—of that very universe. His own fictive discourse could imply a nontraditional fiction, but since his novel was not intended or designed as a utilitarian, communicative, or historical text, he knew that it was not likely to be taken as an injunction to act. He could propose a shattering of old icons, and he could even represent such iconoclasm in literary form. Ultimately, however, it was men and women governed by traditional images who had the power to dispose.

Though Dunbar's freedom in creating *The Sport of the Gods* was shaped by the conventions of the "institution of literature," his novel's rich implications suggest a need for modes of interpretation that go beyond traditional historico-social critical approaches to narrative. In order to apprehend the turn-of-the-century Afro-American narrative as an act of fictive discourse which initiates, in energetic blues ways, a dream of American form, one must engage the freedom of an adequate critical mythology. One's mode of explaining the novel's meanings (and, indeed, the meanings of Afro-American literary texts in general) must transcend, that is to say, a customary, sharply limiting critical strategy that yokes the analysis of works of verbal art to acts of historical interpretation.

Houston A. Baker, Jr., "The 'Limitless' Freedom of Myth: Paul Laurence Dunbar's *The Sport of the Gods* and the Criticism of Afro-American Literature," *Blues, Ideology, and Afro-American Literature: A Vernacular Theory* (Chicago: University of Chicago Press, 1984), pp. 124–25, 137–38

◈ Bibliography

Oak and Ivy. 1893.

Majors and Minors. 1895.

Lyrics of Lowly Life. 1896.

African Romances (with Samuel Coleridge-Taylor). 1897.

Folks from Dixie. 1898.

The Uncalled. 1898.

Dream Lovers. 1898.

Lyrics of the Hearthside. 1899.

Poems of Cabin and Field. 1899.

The Strength of Gideon and Other Stories. 1900.

The Love of Landry. 1900.

Uncle Eph's Christmas: A One Act Negro Musical Sketch (with Will Marion Cook). 1900.

The Fanatics. 1901.

Candle-Lightin' Time. 1901.

The Sport of the Gods. 1902.

Lyrics of Love and Laughter. 1902.

In Old Plantation Days. 1903.

When Malindy Sings. 1903.

The Heart of Happy Hollow. 1904.

Li'l' Gal. 1904.

Lyrics of Sunshine and Shadow. 1905.

Howdy, Honey, Howdy. 1905.

A Plantation Portrait. 1905.

Joggin' Erlong. 1906.

Chris'mus Is a'Comin' and Other Poems. 1907.

Life and Works. Ed. Lina Keck Wiggins. 1907.

Complete Poems. 1913.

Speakin' o' Christmas and Other Christmas and Special Poems. 1914.

Best Stories. Ed. Benjamin Brawley. 1938.

Little Brown Baby: Poems for Young People. Ed. Bertha Rodgers. 1940.

The Paul Laurence Dunbar Reader. Ed. Jay Martin and Gossie H. Hudson. 1975.

I Greet the Dawn. Ed. Ashley Bryan. 1978.

Sutton E. Griggs
1872–1930

SUTTON ELBERT GRIGGS was born in 1872 in Chatfield, Texas. He was edu-cated in schools in Dallas and attended Bishop College in Marshall, Texas. He then attended Richmond Theological Seminary in Richmond, Virginia, graduating in 1893. Ordained as a Baptist minister, he held pastorates in Virginia, Tennessee, and Texas, most notably at the Tabernacle Baptist Church in Memphis.

Griggs achieved early fame with five polemical novels published between 1899 and 1908. *Imperium in Imperio* (1899), perhaps his best-known work, is a sort of political fantasy centering around two individuals, Belton Pied-mont and the mulatto Bernard Belgrave. Both men become leading figures in the Imperium, a separate political state within the United States run by blacks. Bernard, although favorably treated in youth because of his white father, becomes the militant president of the Imperium, while Belton, although discriminated against as a young man, adopts a more accommodat-ing stance. Belton is nevertheless Griggs's mouthpiece for emphasizing the manifold inequities suffered by blacks in the United States.

Griggs's next four novels were all published by the Orion Publishing Company in Nashville. *Overshadowed* (1901) treats of the harsh conditions under which blacks live in the United States, subject to wrongful imprison-ment, sexual violation, and lynching. *Unfettered* (1902) is a melodramatic tale of a lovely mulatto woman, Morlene, who falls in love with a brave young black man, Dorlan Worthell; she agrees to marry him if he can devise a means to "unfetter" the black race. This plan, "Dorlan's Plan," is printed as an appendix to the novel, and proposes to elevate the black race by means of property ownership, education, and the elimination of poverty. *The Hindered Hand* (1905) is a direct response to the negrophobic novels of Thomas Dixon, Jr., author of *The Leopard's Spots* (1902) and *The Clansman* (1905). It deals with the tragic fate of a black family victimized by vicious and prejudiced white gangs. *Pointing the Way* (1908) is a somewhat confused novel in which the characters debate whether blacks should marry within their own race or, as one character believes, seek to eliminate their blackness by marrying whites.

After writing his novels—which, as Oscar Micheaux would do shortly afterwards, Griggs himself sold door to door—Griggs turned to the writing of social and political tracts. The first of these volumes were *The Needs of the South* (1909) and *The Race Question in a New Light* (1909; greatly expanded in 1911 as *Wisdom's Call*). Around 1914 Griggs founded the Public Welfare League as a mouthpiece for black concerns, and it issued some of his works: *The Story of My Struggles* (1914), a slim autobiography; *How to Rise* (1915); *Life's Demands; or, According to the Law* (1916); *The Reconstruction of the Race* (1917); *Guide to Racial Greatness* (1923); and others. In these volumes Griggs discusses the extension of voting rights to blacks, social and legal protection for black women and children, and the intellectual capacity of the black race; he debates whether blacks and whites should form separate societies, and finally concludes that this is both unwise and impracticable.

Around 1920 Griggs became pastor of the Tabernacle Baptist Church in Memphis. Later he served as a minister in Houston, where he established the National Religious and Civic Institute. He also served as the Secretary of the Education Department of the National Baptist Convention in Nashville. Some sermons on racial issues recorded by Griggs in 1928 have recently come to light. Sutton Griggs died in 1930, and his work suffered neglect until the 1970s, when critics began to resurrect and reassess his novels. Although florid and melodramatic, Griggs's novels are seen as searing exposures of the racial prejudice and violence to which blacks were subject at the turn of the century.

▩ *Critical Extracts*

T. O. FULLER   With a brilliant mind and a ready pen, Doctor Griggs went to the fray in such militant fashion that he was almost termed a radical on racial matters. He was acclaimed as a champion in all sections and his appearances before the sessions of the National Baptist Convention and before the general bodies of other religious groups were occasions of wild demonstrations of enthusiastic approval. As an orator he was charming, as a reasoner he was forceful and logical, heard with pleasure at all times. About 1920, he moved to Memphis, and accepted the pastorate of the

Tabernacle Baptist Church. His numerous publications had drawn heavily upon his financial resources and the unexpected financial problems served to cool his enthusiasm and sober his thought on racial attitudes. Consequently, he became the champion of inter-racial good-will and co-operation and the many books written during his life in Memphis were conciliatory and he soon became known as the "Negro Apostle to the White Race." Many of his best friends could not understand his radical change of front, but they still admired him for his apparent earnestness and sincerity of purpose.

Doctor Griggs wrote numerous pamphlets and books, the most important from the standpoint of scholarship was *Guide to Racial Greatness* (1923). During the period of the great World War, Doctor Griggs was in constant demand as a speaker, in the Liberty Bond and other campaigns. He appeared before the Southern Baptist Convention on many occasions in the interest of the American Baptist Theological Seminary, built and operated jointly by the Southern Baptist Convention and the National Baptist Convention, Inc. His activities had much to do with the building of the Seminary.

Endeavoring to enlarge his program, Doctor Griggs undertook the tremendous task of building a great institutional church at Memphis. Be it said to his credit that he erected the building and began the activities and was halted only by the financial stringency which caused the collapse of many similar ventures. With spirit curbed but unbroken, Doctor Griggs returned to Texas and entered upon the pastorate of a church once held by his sainted father. It was in the midst of new and undeveloped plans that the end came unexpectedly and he went to his reward like the disappearance of a brilliant star on the horizon.

> T. O. Fuller, *History of the Negro Baptists of Tennessee* (Memphis: Hopkins Print Co., 1936), pp. 76–78

HUGH M. GLOSTER   Like *Overshadowed*, *Unfettered* provides a dismal picture of race relations. The opposition of prejudiced Southern whites to the education of the Negro is set forth, and an analysis is made of the motives underlying intimidation and segregation. Especially interesting are the political views of Warthell, who, though distrustful of Democrats because their "chief tenets are the white man's supremacy and exclusiveness in government," nevertheless recognizes no unseverable party ties. In his advocacy of the liberation of the Philippines, moreover, Warthell manifests a worldwide as well as a national concern for the advancement of darker races.

As a statement of racial policy, however, the most important section of *Unfettered* is the appended essay called "Dorlan's Plan: Sequel to *Unfettered*: A Dissertation on the Race Problem." This essay, which is a serious approach to the problem of racial adjustment in the United States, points out that the major task is to institute merit and not color as the standard of preferment. Since the oppression of the Negro stems from unfortunate circumstances of the past, the race is urged to "meet and combat the timorous conservatism that has hitherto impeded our progress." The Negro is advised not to rely wholly upon the Republican Party. Listed as necessary in the task of preparing the race for a better future are character development, worthy home life, public school education for the masses, technological institutions for the training of industrial workers, and universities for the development of "men capable of interpreting and influencing world movements, men able to adjust the race to any new conditions that may arise." Land ownership and a back-to-the-farm movement are recommended. Good government and simple justice, not race supremacy and partisan patronage, are defined as the desirable goals of Negro political action. The cultivation of the friendship of the white South as well as of the moral support of other sections of the country and of other civilized nations is also emphasized as a *sine qua non* of enlightened racial policy. In the promotion of this program the support of the orator, journalist, literary artist, painter, sculptor, and composer is solicited. As a statement of desirable procedure for the colored people of the United States, "Dorlan's Plan" is a forerunner of James Weldon Johnson's *Negro Americans, What Now?* (1934) and numerous other guides to interracial harmony in the United States.

Hugh M. Gloster, "Sutton E. Griggs: Novelist of the New Negro," *Phylon* 4, No. 4 (Fourth Quarter 1943): 340–41

S. P. FULLINWINDER   Griggs was a novelist of sorts who found in conscious escape the only alternative to the impossible situation of being locked out of the society to which he belonged. He was a minor figure at best. A lifelong resident of the South, he was one of the few southerners to join and actively participate in the militant Niagara Movement. He was something of a religious modernist. And, though not a scholar in any formal sense, he was in close touch with the most advanced social thought. He toyed with the religiously acceptable ideas of Herbert Spencer and Benjamin Kidd until he decided that honesty demanded a more literally materialistic interpretation of Darwin. For a clergyman buried away deep in the Bible belt this kind of rugged intellectual honesty is astonishing. Life could not have been easy. As if religious radicalism were not enough, he kept abreast of, and propounded, the most modern American social thought, rejecting the work ethic of Booker T. Washington in favor of environmental determinism. He was well acquainted with the work in psychology done by Edward T. Thorndike, whose "law of effect" (latterly known as "reinforcement") was to be one of the building blocks of American behaviorism and its corollary that the human personality is a mirror of the culture around it. He quoted Rousseau, J. S. Huxley and William E. Locking in support of his own mature contention that social environment is all in the life of man. From this he drew the old socialist conclusion, that by controlling their social environment men can make themselves better. A civil rights activist in the South; a Darwinist within the Negro clergy; a socialist swimming against the current of Washington's rugged individualism—all these things define Griggs as a man of large courage. But where the problems of identity intruded he fled in panic.

> S. P. Fullinwinder, *The Mind and Mood of Black America: 20th Century Thought* (Homewood, IL: Dorsey Press, 1969), pp. 73–74

ROBERT E. FLEMING   ⟨. . .⟩ Griggs' techniques ⟨in *Imperium in Imperio*⟩ perform different but complementary functions. His dramatic and authorial expositions of racial injustice are both informative and effective; they are designed to appeal to the white reader's sense of fair play as well as to win sympathy for black people. His comic scenes not only relieve the generally somber tone of the novel but also further the author's cause: Griggs attempts to change undesirable attitudes of whites by showing readers how ridiculous it is for people to feel superior merely because of their race. Still another approach, similar in some ways to the methods of the Black Panther Party of our day, is the appeal to fear. It is the use of this approach that has created misunderstanding about Griggs. Like Sam Greenlee in his recent novel *The Spook Who Sat by the Door* (1969), Griggs uses realistic and concrete details to give substance to an essentially fantastic vision. In order to achieve a frightening prophetic effect, both Greenlee and Griggs use hyperbole; by exaggerating possible reactions of blacks to injustice, they attempt to convince the reader that immediate reforms are imperative if the nightmare of black revolution is to be averted.

In his appeal to the reader's fear, Griggs foreshadows the introduction of the Imperium by pointing out causes for growing discontent. For example, he notes that black college graduates like Belton Piedmont find themselves educated but unemployable: "They grew to hate a flag that would float in an undisturbed manner over such a condition of affairs. They began to abuse and execrate a national government that would not protect them against color prejudice, but on the contrary actually practiced it itself." Such conditions lead men to join the Imperium, a secret government which made "use of all [the] secret orders already formed by negroes" and which was founded "to secure protection for their lives and the full enjoyment of all rights and privileges due American citizens." To make the Imperium seem real and believable, Griggs presents in detail the society's history, organization, financing, and procedures. However, under the leadership of Bernard Belgrave, Piedmont's boyhood rival, the society becomes more militant. In his first speech as president of the Imperium, Belgrave stirs the anger of the members by reminding them of the suffering they have undergone as a race—slavery, exclusion from good jobs, deprivation of civil rights, inferior education, unfair treatment in the courts, and the horrors of mob rule. He asks how blacks are to obtain freedom. Amalgamation with the white race and emigration to Africa are both rejected. Finally, a speaker rises "to stick a match to the powder magazine which Belgrave had left uncovered in all their bosoms." He favors war, and his suggestion is enthusiastically accepted.

At this point Belton Piedmont, second only to Belgrave in the Imperium hierarchy, rises to dissent. In a twenty-page speech he argues that conditions are not as bad as Belgrave has suggested and that since emancipation conditions have been better. He urges a course of action he feels will achieve their goals without bloodshed: revelation of the Imperium's existence; warning that its members intend to gain their rights; and, if these means fail, the peaceful move of all black people to the state of Texas, where their numbers will enable them to control the state government. The forces that favor war win, and Piedmont, who refuses to condone premeditated mass murder, is executed.

Thus, Griggs uses the Imperium plot as the most powerful weapon in his attack on racial injustice; he resorts to fear in order to motivate those readers who have not been moved by reason, sympathy, or laughter. Although the Imperium plot is fantastic, Griggs bases it on facts: the large number of black people in the United States; their growing discontent; and the Anglo-Saxons' chronic underestimation of the Negro character. However, the novel is neither a blueprint nor a call to violence; indeed, Griggs' use of Belton Piedmont as his hero, rather than the more militant Bernard Belgrave, indicates where his true sympathy lies. The note on which the novel ends provides further evidence of Griggs' viewpoint. One of the members, Bert Trout, has been influenced by Piedmont's plea for peace and exposes the plot with the warning that crushing the Imperium will only postpone the inevitable racial holocaust unless its root causes are eradicated: "I only ask as a return [for this disclosure] that all mankind will join hands and help my poor downtrodden people to secure those rights for which they organized the Imperium. . . . I urge this because love of liberty is such an inventive genius, that if you destroy one device it at once constructs another more powerful." Surely Bert Trout speaks for the author in these closing lines of the novel.

Robert E. Fleming, "Sutton E. Griggs: Militant Black Novelist," *Phylon* 34, No. 1 (March 1973): 75–77

JUDITH R. BERZON   Violence is rejected throughout Griggs's works, as is any action that could be construed as traitorous to the Republic. In *The Hindered Hand*, Griggs employs the character of Gus Martin in order to repudiate violent black nationalism. Like Earl Bluefield, the light-skinned radical protagonist of *The Hindered Hand*, whose ideas are pitted against those of dark-skinned, conservative Ensal Ellwood, Gus is presented sympathetically, but his ideas are rejected nonetheless. He is described as ordinarily being tractable, but his attitudes are changing. On one occasion, he "questioned the existence of God, and, begging pardon, asserted that the Gospel was the Negro's greatest curse, that it unmanned the race. As for the United States government, he said, 'The flag ain't any more to me than any other dirty rag.'" Griggs describes Gus as a child of the new race philosophy which holds that each individual should resent the injustices put upon him and should kill the enemy. He is murdered while pursuing this policy.

In addition to the violent means Earl suggests for making white Americans aware of the Negro's plight and the conditions under which they live— a plan that is naturally rejected by Ensal—Griggs gives his conservative protagonist a further opportunity to demonstrate his loyalty to the United States government. A certain Mr. Hostility (!) comes to visit Ensal and explains that he is implacably opposed to the worldwide domination of the Anglo-Saxon race. He wants to enable the Slav peoples to have this power and asks Ensal to help him. Hostility has a jar filled with yellow fever germs, to which the Negro is immune, and wants Ensal to help him release them. Southern whites will die by the millions; Ensal is appalled.

In *Pointing the Way*, Baug Peppers says that he is "a patriot. I love the South. I would like to see the South take its old-time place in the councils of the nation." Even in *Imperium in Imperio*, the novel in which the most radical ideas are considered, violence and treason are rejected. Bernard, leader of the Imperium in Imperio, suggests a plan (which everyone but

Belton accepts) to seize Austin, Texas; destroy the United States Navy if necessary; and, having entered into secret negotiations with the enemies of the United States, demand the surrender of Texas and Louisiana. Belton says that Bernard's plan is treason: he loves the Union and the South and could die as his forefathers did, fighting for his country's honor. He says that "love of country is one of the deepest passions in the human bosom."

Although these characters reject violence as a solution to the race problem, they do not remain silent on the subject of repression by the powers that be. In *The Hindered Hand*, Ensal Ellwood speaks out against repression, and says that it is unfortunately "the order of the day, and [since] the process of the survival of the fittest [is] operating . . . that man who best exemplifies the repressive faculty will survive in the political warfare." Earl Bluefield also addresses himself to this issue and combines an attack on industrial education and conservative ideology at the same time that he attacks repression by white society: "How great an army of carpenters can hammer the spirit of repression out of those who hold that the eternal repression of the Negro is the nation's only safeguard?"

Judith R. Berzon, *Neither White Nor Black: The Mulatto Character in American Fiction* (New York: New York University Press, 1978), pp. 209–11

ARLENE A. ELDER   Griggs was clearly in agreement with W. E. B. Du Bois's contention that economic success without political power is an illusory hope upon which to rest racial progress. Among his minor characters, there are many spokesmen for types of political action that Griggs rejects. It is never clear whether he takes seriously Viola Martin's concern ⟨in *Imperium in Imperio*⟩ that intermarriage between Blacks and whites or mulattoes produces sterility and "devitalization" in the race. But he obviously views racial purity as essential to the Blacks' struggle. When Ensal leaves for Africa, his primary concern is to impress the importance of this view upon his brothers: "Fellow Negroes, for the sake of world interests, it is my hope that you will maintain your ambition for racial purity. So long as your blood relationship to Africa is apparent to you the world has a redeeming source specially equipped for the work of the uplift of that continent." The view that dark-skinned Blacks must marry those fairer than themselves is clearly scored in *Overshadowed* in the satiric condemnation of the self-destructive foibles of the middle class. Mrs. Seabright's secretive corollary to this plan, her desire to infiltrate the ranks of unsuspecting whites, thereby eventually taking over southern institutions, leads to much of the violence in *The Hindered Hand*—her son's murder, one daughter's madness, another's disinheritance, her husband's disappearance, and her own suicide. Miss Letitia in *Pointing the Way* is scarcely more successful. 〈. . .〉

Griggs's political narratives, then, set the stage for modern racial analysis and symbolic interpretations of the African-American experience. Moreover, they provide Black literature's first portrait of independent Blacks who are neither traditional figures nor counterstereotypes. Despite his pieties, Belton Piedmont is closer in temperament and fate to the hero of John Williams's *Man Who Cried I Am* (1967) than he is to William Wells Brown's Jerome or Frank Webb's Mr. Walters.

Arlene A. Elder, "Sutton Griggs: The Dilemma of the Black Bourgeoisie," *The "Hindered Hand": Cultural Implications of Early African-American Fiction* (Westport, CT: Greenwood Press, 1978), pp. 101–3

JAMES ROBERT PAYNE   The persuasiveness and strength of Griggs's *Imperium in Imperio*, especially its imaginative concluding section, derive to a significant degree from Griggs's adept use of immediate historical contextual materials. Griggs locates his vividly imagined militant black organization, the Imperium, near Waco, Texas, in what to outward appearance is Thomas Jefferson College, Griggs's ironic nod to an earlier American revolutionary thinker, one who tried to ban slavery while keeping slaves himself. The leaders of the Imperium, like many American blacks of the time in fact, took an interest in the Cuban nationalist insurrection which preceded the Spanish-American War because, as the narrator states, "the Cubans were in a large measure negroes."

When the United States Congress met in April 1898 to consider resolutions that would result in war with Spain, the Congress of the Imperium, like a "shadow" government, met in special session to consider what should be its attitude "to this Anglo-Saxon race, which calls upon us to defend the fatherland and at the same moment treats us in a manner to make us execrate it." While the Imperium shares the concerns of the United States Congress regarding the supposed attack on the Maine and with helping Cuba gain independence, the black leadership is also concerned with the murder of one of its members, Felix A. Cook, whose seat in the meeting hall remains dramatically vacant and is draped in black. In developing the figure of Cook, Griggs clearly draws on the contemporary incident of the murder of Frazier B. Baker. Griggs's Cook, like Baker, was appointed postmaster of Lake City, South Carolina, by President McKinley. And as in the antecedent Baker case, Cook was assassinated by a local mob which could not stand the idea of a black man as a postmaster.

Because the Frazier Baker murder is well-documented, we can observe just how Griggs reworks the historical material for integration into his fiction. Most remarkable is how Griggs, though writing a novel of black militancy and protest, actually tones down the attack on the postmaster and his family. In the actual case, not only the postmaster but also his infant son were killed by the mob. In Griggs's fictional representation only the postmaster is killed. Griggs wants to present the horrors of American racism to his readers, yet he omits a most gruesome detail of his historical material antecedent to the scene. Perhaps Griggs believed that his black readership, which was well-established, would not care to have every abhorrent detail of the lynching rehearsed, the likes of which would be already too well-known in the Afroamerican community of the day. And perhaps Griggs intuited that if he offered the full truth, many not of or not directly conversant with the Afroamerican community would turn away in disbelief. Ironically, a fuller presentation of what actually happened, including the shooting of the infant, might have made the novel seem "unrealistic" and exaggerated to some readers. In short, if he had used more of the grotesque actual detail of the Baker lynching, Griggs might have lost some of his readers to his essential truth. ⟨. . .⟩

If we read *Imperium in Imperio* as working in tension with Afroamerican historical phenomena, we see that Griggs is projecting in his fiction a potential radical alternative to a "loyal" black response to the Spanish-American War. What if those black citizens who had helped America acquire an empire from Spain had joined with the foreign adversary to force the United States to cede to a black Imperium two of its states? Appearing a few months after the important black role in the Spanish-American War was acknowledged in special ceremonies and in newspaper accounts across the country, *Imperium in Imperio* challenges readers with the idea that black Americans have the potential of playing a different sort of role in a foreign war than they did in 1898.

James Robert Payne, "Griggs and Corrothers: Historical Reality and Black Fiction," *Explorations in Ethnic Studies* 6, No. 1 (January 1983): 3–5

JANE CAMPBELL   Griggs especially strives to awaken his audience to blacks' innate power; his notion of black solidarity, autonomy, and separatism cemented by creative thinkers conjoins the myth of the messiah with his faith in Western rationality. His saviors must unite their intellectual and visionary capacities to deliver Afro-America from its sense of powerlessness, effect political change, and, ultimately, reorder the world. For Griggs, post-

Reconstruction's overwhelming constraints on black America dictate identification with transcendent figures, for suffering and death constitute everyday realities. Although Griggs's ideal leadership rests on an educational foundation, he insists that black thinkers must not forget their folk roots or seek to assimilate. In keeping with such thinking, he jettisons Brown's reverence for light skin, encouraging pride in blackness. Given the dangers implicit in Griggs's endorsement of revolt, however, his dramatization of revolt divides in two, and one of his messiahs becomes an accommodationist.

Griggs employs a number of strategies in the mythmaking process. Romance, his primary device, serves him well for projecting his utopian vision of black political power embodied in a gigantic secret society designed to rectify social injustice. His heroes and heroines occupy the upper reaches of human possibility, hovering close to divinities in their abilities to survive attempts on their lives, and in their intellectual and artistic talents, qualities that occasion instant stardom. Just as the romance allows for characters of ideological rather than psychological magnitude, so too does romance plotting free the narrative from the burden of verisimilitude. His heroes' talents enable them to unify Afro-America, creating a national organization that exceeds the limits of plausibility in size and power. To elucidate his allegiance to blackness, Griggs designs a subplot in which one of his heroines commits suicide rather than produce light-skinned children with her suitor. To dramatize the healing power of laughter, Griggs makes use of the oral narrative mode, reinforcing trickster figures' centrality in black life. Aside from his reliance on Sentimental Heroines, the Genteel Tradition and inflated diction, Griggs has trouble incorporating historical events into his narrative, and he repudiates African historical connections. Despite his limitations, however, Griggs remains the first black artist to dramatize an appreciation of dark skin and political separatism and as such anticipates later historical fiction.

Jane Campbell, "A Necessary Ambivalence: Sutton Griggs's *Imperium in Imperio* and Charles Chesnutt's *The Marrow of Tradition*," *Mythic Black Fiction: The Transformation of History* (Knoxville: University of Tennessee Press, 1986), pp. 42–43

STEVEN C. TRACY   Two of Griggs' sermons ⟨recorded in 1928⟩ deal with racial disharmony, and the actions that define heroes in Griggs' stories reveal, once again, a middle-class approach to racial matters though, as ⟨Paul⟩ Oliver points out, "A Hero Closes a War" was "almost alone among recorded sermons in making any specific reference to racial tension." The heroes of "Saving the Day" accomplish what history, science, and governments cannot by selflessly offering themselves as "temporary sand bags" to stop the rush of water. By comparing this group of "Negroes" to the priests of the Israelites, Griggs seems to be seeking to prove the worthiness of "the Negro" through these people. Griggs avoids the fact that, very often, in flood times blacks were pressed into service on levees and forced to work until they dropped, as described in Richard Wright's "Down by the Riverside," which could have taken its setting from the 1927 flooding of the Mississippi River. That flood, the river's worst flood disaster in recorded history, happened the year before Griggs' recordings. Given this circumstance, their willingness to sacrifice their lives to save lives and crops seems an effort to prove their "nobility." Like his depiction of his hero in "A Hero Closes a War," this heroic action involves the self-sacrifice of some blacks to save everyone else, and the language describing the storm is elevated and "literary," personifying the river.

Racial conflict is more obvious in "A Hero Closes a War" in the actions of whites to prevent blacks from regaining their positions in a capsized boat. Although the story implies that whites and blacks were all "in the same boat" at one time, it still suggests that it is the "Negro's" responsibility to sacrifice, to prove his worthiness so that he may be accepted by the offending whites. Griggs has no problem with this circumstance, or with the implication that two whites must be saved before one "Negro." He anticipates that there may be some criticism of this attitude, recognizing that some "Negroes" might call his hero a traitor to his race and some whites might still not be appeased, but he insists that the self-sacrifice is for the common good. He never mentions any necessity for whites to act decently in the first place. However, it is very interesting that Griggs acknowledges a racial war that coincided with World War I, that was amplified as white and black soldiers fought, in this case, side by side. In fact, Griggs gets a bit ambiguous when he discusses this. After "the race war was over," he discusses the feeling of the "fellows" toward the swimmer, who they might have considered a traitor to his race "because of the war that was raging." To which war was Griggs referring: the World War, the race war, or the private war between the two groups of soldiers? It is likely that Griggs was referring to the last of these, but the ambiguity might suggest unrest because of the World War as well. Finally, it should be noted that these two "racial" sermons were not released on the same 78 RPM record. Rather, each sermon was coupled with a "non-racial" one despite the fact that the racial sermons were recorded on the same day. Perhaps this indicates a hesitancy to release a record that deals too extensively with racial subjects; perhaps it indicates a desire to capitalize on the subjects of the sermons on two records instead of one. The reason behind the pairings will probably never be definitely known.

Finally, these recordings reflect Griggs' growing preoccupation with racial cooperation that involved the potential loss of African-American lives, pride, and style. The burden of proof, of being worthy of the respect of whites, resided with blacks who could treat themselves as inanimate objects (sand bags), aid those who denied them safety and equality, and imitate the manners of speech and performance that would help "legitimize" them in the eyes of whites. If Griggs was praying for racial cooperation, the surprise answer he most likely would have got from many whites would not have been the idealized one he presented in "A Hero Closes a War," but a resounding "no." He seems to have been willing to endure that patiently until it changed.

> Steven C. Tracy, "Saving the Day: The Recordings of the Reverend Sutton E. Griggs," *Phylon* 47, No. 1 (June 1986): 165–66

◈ *Bibliography*

Imperium in Imperio. 1899.

Overshadowed. 1901.

Unfettered. 1902.

The Hindered Hand; or, The Reign of the Repressionist. 1905.

The One Great Question . . . 1907.

Pointing the Way. 1908.

Needs of the South. 1909.

The Race Question in a New Light. 1909.

Wisdom's Call. 1911.

The Story of My Struggles. 1914.

How to Rise. 1915.

Life's Demands; or, According to the Law. 1916.

The Reconstruction of a Race. 1917.

Light on Racial Issues. 1921.

Science of Collective Efficiency. 1921.

Guide to Racial Greatness; or, The Science of Collective Efficiency. 1923.

The Negro's Next Step. 1923.

Kingdom Builders' Manual: Companion Book to Guide to Racial Greatness. 1924.

Paths of Progress; or, Co-operation between the Races. 1925.

Triumph of the Simple Virtues; or, The Life Story of John L. Webb. c. 1926.

The Winning Policy. 1927.

◈ ◈ ◈

Pauline E. Hopkins
1859–1930

PAULINE ELIZABETH HOPKINS was born in 1859 in Portland, Maine, the daughter of Northrup and Sarah Allen Hopkins. Shortly after her birth her parents moved to Boston, where she attended the public schools. At fifteen she won a writing contest sponsored by William Wells Brown and the Congregational Publishing Society on the theme of temperance.

Hopkins's first literary work was a play, *Slaves' Escape; or, The Underground Railroad*, written in 1879 and produced the next year by a touring group organized by her family, the Hopkins' Colored Troubadours, in which her mother, her stepfather, and Hopkins herself acted. The play was later published as *Peculiar Sam; or, The Underground Railroad*, although the date of publication is not known. Hopkins earned considerable renown as an actress and singer, acquiring the nickname "Boston's Favorite Soprano." She also wrote at least one further play, *One Scene from the Drama of Early Days*, but it was apparently never performed and the manuscript is now lost.

Around 1892 Hopkins enrolled in a stenography course and earned her livelihood in this profession for several years, working for four years at the Bureau of Statistics. In 1900 the founding of the *Colored American* magazine changed the course of her career and her writing. She began writing voluminously for the magazine, and by the second issue had joined its staff. Her earliest work for it was a short story, "The Mystery within Us," published in the magazine's first issue (May 1900).

Hopkins's one separately published novel, *Contending Forces: A Romance Illustrative of Negro Life North and South,* was issued in 1900 by the Colored Co-operative Publishing Company, the publisher of *Colored American.* This historical romance of a love affair between a mulatto, Will Smith, and an octoroon, Sappho Clark, is a powerful examination of the life of black women within white society, and touches upon many fundamental issues of black social life. Although it employs many of the conventions of the popular sentimental romance of the period, it probes such concerns as the sexual exploitation of black women, the searing effects of slavery, the need for strong family ties, and other matters.

The *Colored American* also serialized three novels by Hopkins: *Hagar's Daughter: A Story of Southern Caste Prejudice* (March 1901–March 1902); *Winona: A Tale of Negro Life in the South and Southwest* (May–October 1902); and *Of One Blood; or, The Hidden Self* (November 1902–November 1903). *Hagar's Daughter*, published under the pseudonym Sarah A. Allen, is the story of a woman, Hagar, who is married to a Southern white planter and discovers that she has black ancestry; the novel treats of her and her daughter's attempts to come to terms with their blackness. *Winona* deals with a woman born of a white man who becomes the chief of an Indian tribe and a fugitive slave woman. Winona goes to England with her British lover in the hope of escaping prejudice. In *Of One Blood* Reuel Briggs, about to commit suicide because he is black, is rescued by a light-skinned black singer, Dianthe Lusk; Reuel himself then resuscitates Dianthe after a train accident and marries her, but she is stolen from him by his white friend Aubrey Livingston, who rapes and kills her. In the end it is revealed that Reuel, Dianthe, and Aubrey all have a common mother and are therefore "of one blood." These three novels have been collected in *The Magazine Novels of Pauline E. Hopkins* (1988).

In addition to fiction, Hopkins wrote a considerable amount of nonfiction and journalism for the *Colored American*. A series of articles entitled "Famous Men of the Negro Race" (February 1901–September 1902) dealt with such figures as Frederick Douglass and William Wells Brown, while "Famous Women of the Negro Race" (November 1901–October 1902) discussed Sojourner Truth, Harriet Tubman, Frances E. W. Harper, and others.

By 1904 Hopkins had become too ill to work on the magazine. She continued writing, however, and published a series, "The Dark Races of the Twentieth Century," in *Voice of the Negro* (February–July 1905). She herself published a treatise, *A Primer of Facts Pertaining to the Greatness of Africa* (1905). This was, however, the last of her major writings, aside from a novelette, "Topsy Templeton," published in 1916 in *New Era*.

Hopkins resumed her stenographic work, being employed by the Massachusetts Institute of Technology. She died as a result of a freak accident on August 13, 1930. Her work suffered critical neglect until the 1970s, when *Contending Forces* was hailed as a pioneering work of black American fiction. Her short stories and journalism, however, remain uncollected.

◈ *Critical Extracts*

ANN ALLEN SHOCKLEY   By November, 1903, ⟨Hopkins⟩ had
become Literary Editor of the *Colored American*. Much of her personal time
and effort was now spent in promoting the magazine. For example, in
January, 1904, she was one of the founders of the Colored American League
in Boston (fictionalized in a chapter of her *Contending Forces* as "The
American Colored League")—an organization comprised of "some twenty
or more representative ladies and gentlemen of the colored citizens of
Boston" ⟨*Colored American*, March 1904⟩ which helped sustain the *Colored
American* during the summer months in a series of public meetings over the
country to gain interest and support for the magazine.

  Miss Hopkins's spirit and love for the magazine were demonstrated as
well by her prolific contributions to it. Six of her short stories appeared in
the publication, among these "Talma Gordon," "George Washington: A
Christmas Story," and "Bro'r Abr'm Jimson's Wedding. A Christmas Story."
Two short novels which dealt with interracial love were also serialized in
the *Colored American*. The first one, *Winona: A Tale of Negro Life in the
South and Southwest in the 1840's*, was serialized in twenty-four chapters.
Winona was the daughter of a white man in Buffalo, New York, who joined
an Indian tribe and became its chief. The chief married a fugitive slave girl
who died while giving birth to Winona. The plot was sensational and
complicated, filled with adventurous escapades, murder, and romance. In
the conclusion, Winona and her white English lover go to England where
the "American caste prejudice could not touch them beyond the sea." Her
second short novel, *Of One Blood or The Hidden Self*, began serializing in
the October, 1902 issue immediately following the conclusion of *Winona*.
It was a similarly complicated tale of interracial romance, and filled with
the mysticism of the mind and spirit.

  The recurring theme of interracial love in Miss Hopkins's serials was
noted by a white reader, Cornelia A. Condict, who wrote a letter to the
editor saying: "Without exception, they have been of love between the
colored and white. Does that mean that your novelists can imagine no love
beautiful and sublime within the range of the colored race, for each other?"
Miss Hopkins replied to this with candor while stating the basic philosophy
of her fiction:

> . . . My stories are definitely planned to show the obstacles
> persistently placed in our paths by a dominant race to subjugate us
> spiritually. Marriage is made illegal between the races and the

mulattoes increase. Thus the shadow of corruption falls on
the blacks and on the whites, without whose aid the mulattoes
would not exist.

Ann Allen Shockley, "Pauline Elizabeth Hopkins: A Biographical Excursion into
Obscurity," *Phylon* 33, No. 1 (Spring 1972): 24–25

CLAUDIA TATE   The structure of ⟨*Winona*⟩ conforms to basic
conventions. But *Winona* is even more sensational than *Contending Forces*
in that there are more incredible coincidences, swashbuckling adventures,
and exaggerated heroic descriptions, all held together with a very sentimental
love story. Winona's appearance, as we might expect, conforms to the tragic
mulatto mold: "Her wide brow, about which the hair clustered in dark rings,
the beautifully chiselled features, the olive complexion with a hint of pink."
And her hero, Maxwell, is equally as handsome, though fair: ". . . a slender,
well-knit figure with a bright, handsome face, blue eyes and a mobile mouth
slightly touched with down on his upper lip." The virtuous pair are rewarded
with prosperity and happiness, while the villain suffers a painful death.

Hopkins placed this novel into the genre of the fugitive slave story and
identified her protest as that against the arbitrary segregation and subjection
of black Americans:

> Many strange tales of romantic happenings in this mixed
> community of Anglo-Saxons, Indians and Negroes might be
> told similar to the one I am about to relate, and the world stand
> aghast and may try to find the dividing line supposed to be
> a natural barrier between the whites and the dark-skinned race.

Thus, as is the case with *Contending Forces,* the central issue of *Winona* is
its protest against racial injustice, but unlike *Contending Forces, Winona*
outlines no program of social reform other than that offered by escape.
Whereas escape offered a possible resolution to the slave's dilemma prior to
1864, Hopkins's contemporary scene of 1901 afforded virtually no ostensible
reason for her to write an abolitionist novel. Perhaps she wrote the novel
as an exercise in nostalgia, intended to arouse sympathy for oppressed black
Americans. There was, however, more than sufficient reason to condemn
the practices of employment and housing discrimination, separate public
accommodations, mob violence, and lynching, as she had done in *Contending
Forces.* Whereas her first novel was very sensitive to the racial issues of 1900
and consequently addressed each of them, *Winona* seems to be essentially an
escapist, melodramatic romance in which Hopkins used sentimental love
as a means for supporting an appeal for racial justice. Though, granted,

Hopkins does dramatize the fact that being black in America means being subjected to racial abuse, she offers little hope to those who cannot escape like Winona and Jude.

Women's issues, which were central to the argument of *Contending Forces*, have been abandoned entirely in *Winona*. Although marriage is depicted as woman's ambition in both *Contending Forces* and *Winona*, in the latter novel a woman's role is seen exclusively as finding a suitable husband and tending to his needs. Love is translated singularly into duty, and duty finds expression only on the domestic front. We do not see women, like Mrs. Willis of *Contending Forces*, who are their husbands' helpmates in the struggle for racial advancement. On the contrary, marriage offers women its own blissful escape in *Winona*, and marital love is portrayed as the balm which soothes their worldly wounds. When we turn our attention to the subject of the advancement of black women, we find no discussion of this topic at all. Although Hopkins was, nevertheless, a product of the nineteenth century's rising consciousness of women's concerns, it is surprising to find that this issue appears so inconsistently in her work.

> Claudia Tate, "Pauline Hopkins: Our Literary Foremother," *Conjuring: Black Women, Fiction, and Literary Tradition*, ed. Marjorie Pryse and Hortense J. Spillers (Bloomington: Indiana University Press, 1985), pp. 60–61

JANE CAMPBELL   *Contending Forces* fictionalizes women's collective efforts to create a countermythology. In the chapter entitled "The Sewing Circle," a large group of women gather to make garments for a church fair. Mrs. Willis, who plays a significant role in this chapter, serves as the embodiment of the black women's club movement. Although women's organizations existed before the Civil War, during the 1890s these clubs, led by such esteemed members as Frances Harper, Mary Church Terrell, and Fannie Barrier Williams, achieved greater prominence than they had earlier, in part because of the formation of the National Association of Colored Women in 1896. Gerda Lerner notes that it is unclear whether this association spawned new clubs or whether existing clubs began to attain recognition; nevertheless, the club movement as a whole deserves credit for uniting black women in the crusades against lynching and Jim Crow and for integration. When characters in the sewing circle discuss woman's role in racial upbuilding, they turn to Mrs. Willis for direction. Mrs. Willis echoes Harper's injunction that mothers, as culture bearers, constitute black America's future, and she applauds African women's native virtue, suggesting that black American women, by extension, are innately virtuous. She goes on to caution her listeners that black women must not assume responsibility for the sexual exploitation of their ancestors and themselves. With this chapter, Harper charts black woman's role in changing history through her solidarity with other women, who help her to forge a new vision that runs counter to the one white culture promulgates. At the same time, the cult of domesticity, a motif pervading *Contending Forces*, enshrines the possibilities inherent in the home, where a sewing circle can become a political forum.

Hopkins's concept of history, exhibited in the aforementioned chapter and elsewhere, presupposes an educated, "cultured" class of leaders who will foster the rest of Afro-America so that it may evolve into ideal humanity. Patronizing as her mythmaking seems, it mirrors the attitudes of other post-Reconstruction black writers in its evolutionary concept of history. Unlike Harper, however, Hopkins conveys no notion that blacks are inherently more moral than whites or that black leaders will enhance white evolution. If anything, Hopkins hazards the idea that racial intermixture with Anglo-Saxons, however much it exploits women, has improved Afro-Americans, infusing blacks with characteristics of "the higher race." This blatant endorsement of racial supremacy has been responsible, in part, for the critical neglect of Hopkins's fiction; whether she was collapsing under the weight of the dominant cultural ideology or merely appealing to a white audience fails to excuse her. Yet paradoxically, Hopkins insists that, regardless of skin color, African descent people must identify with Afro-American. In addition, she avows in her epigraph from Emerson that whites have debased themselves by racial oppression. Finally, *Contending Forces* challenges "the best" of both races to consolidate in order to bring about historical change. Denouncing violence for agitation, Hopkins seeks to arouse moral urgency in black and white readers alike.

Jane Campbell, "Female Paradigms in Frances Harper's *Iola Leroy* and Pauline Hopkins's *Contending Forces*," *Mythic Black Fiction: The Transformation of History* (Knoxville: University of Tennessee Press, 1986), pp. 39–40

HAZEL V. CARBY   What Hopkins concentrated on ⟨in *Contending Forces*⟩ was a representation of the black female body as colonized by white male power and practices; if oppositional control was exerted by a black male, as in the story of Mabelle's father, the black male was destroyed. The link between economic/political power and economic/sexual power was firmly established in the battle for the control over women's bodies. Hopkins repeatedly asserted the importance of the relation between histories: the contemporary rape of black women was linked to the oppression of the female slave. Children were destined to follow the condition of their mothers into a black, segregated realm of existence from where they were unable to challenge the white-controlled structure of property and power. Any economic, political, or social advance made by black men resulted in accusations of a threat to the white female body, the source of heirs to power and property, and subsequent death at the hands of a lynch mob. A desire for a pure black womanhood, an uncolonized black female body, was the false hope of Sappho's pretense. The only possible future for her black womanhood was through a confrontation with, not denial of, her history. The struggle to establish and assert her womanhood was a struggle of redemption: a retrieval and reclaiming of the previously colonized. The reunited Mabelle/Sappho was a representation of a womanhood in which motherhood was not contingent upon wifehood, and Will was a representation of a black manhood that did not demand that women be a medium of economic exchange between men. The figure of Mabelle/Sappho lost her father when he refused to accept that his daughter was a medium of cash exchange with his white stepbrother. Beaubean had his fatherhood denied at the moment when he attempted to assert such patriarchal control and was slaughtered by a white mob. Instead of representing a black manhood that was an equivalent to white patriarchy, Hopkins grasped for the utopian possibility that Will could be a husband/partner to Mabelle/Sappho, when he accepted her sexual history, without having to occupy the space of father to her child.

Contending Forces was the most detailed exploration of the parameters of black womanhood and of the patriarchal limitations of black manhood in Hopkins's fiction. In her following three novels, Hopkins would adopt the more popular conventions of womanhood and manhood that defined heroes and heroines as she produced a magazine fiction that sought a wide audience. Hopkins continued to write popular fiction at the same time as she adopted popular fictional formulas and was the first Afro-American author to produce a black popular fiction that drew on the archetypes of dime novels and story papers.

Hazel V. Carby, " 'Of What Use Is Fiction?': Pauline Elizabeth Hopkins," *Reconstructing Womanhood: The Emergence of the Afro-American Woman Novelist* (New York: Oxford University Press, 1987), pp. 143–44

DICKSON D. BRUCE, JR.   ⟨*Hagar's Daughter*⟩ begins with a version of the tragic mulatto story, as Hagar, the beautiful young wife of a southern planter named Ellis Enson, is discovered to have black ancestry.

In her grief and despair, she jumps with her child from a high bridge crossing the Potomac, apparently to her death. The scene is virtually identical to a similar episode at the conclusion of William Wells Brown's *Clotel*. But Hopkins departed from the usual treatment of the tragic mulatto. Commonly, in such stories, the heroine's tragedy is a result of the sexual hypocrisy of the white man. In Hopkins' story, the element of sexual hypocrisy does not appear. Hagar decides upon suicide because Ellis has apparently died while trying to arrange for their removal to Europe, where they can continue to live openly as husband and wife, away from the prejudices of white America. Like ⟨George Marion⟩ McClellan's "Old Greenbottom Inn," Hopkins' *Hagar's Daughter* held out the possibility of a real interracial love that triumphed over prejudice.

But Hopkins also went a step further than McClellan in her treatment of interracial love. As the word *apparently* in the synopsis indicates, neither Hagar nor Ellis actually dies in the early going of the novel. After spinning a complex tale of Washington intrigue, set twenty years beyond the apparent deaths of husband and wife, Hopkins reunited them through a series of coincidences. Again, Ellis, knowing full well Hagar's background, wants her to be his wife, creating a marriage that makes race irrelevant. The only tragic sidelight is that a young white man in love with Hagar's daughter spurns the girl because of her ancestry. In the end, he sees the error of his ways; but he cannot do anything about it. She has died, the victim of a fever. Here, of course, is the tragic mulatto, but presented in a way—balanced by her parents' unhappiness—that displays the alternative to, rather than the inevitability of, the young girl's tragic end, an alternative that even her misguided young man has come to see.

Hagar's Daughter was a frank espousal of the possibility and rightness of interracial romance. It was like "Talma Gordon" ⟨*Colored American*, October 1900⟩ in this regard, portraying a perspective consistent with but still more fully assimilationist than that of *Contending Forces*. Hopkins recognized that if racial barriers were to be represented as truly possible to overcome, then even the barrier to intermarriage had to be seen as artificial. Critic Claudia Tate has pointed out that marriage as a source of identity and stability was important in all of Hopkins' novels. In *Hagar's Daughter*, Hopkins used interracial marriage to encapsulate a vision of the irrelevance of racial identity in a decent world.

Dickson D. Bruce, Jr., *Black American Writing from the Nadir: The Evolution of a Literary Tradition 1877–1915* (Baton Rouge: Louisiana State University Press, 1989), pp. 150–51

CLAUDIA TATE   Mrs. Willis ⟨in *Contending Forces*⟩ is the principal proponent for the law of the mother. In the chapter entitled "The Sewing Circle," she advises Sappho, on hearing her fictitious version of her personal history. Sappho recalls: "I once knew a woman who had sinned. . . . She married a man who would have despised her had he known her story; but as it is, she is looked upon as a pattern of virtue for all women. . . . Ought she not to have told her husband before marriage? Was it not her duty to have thrown herself upon his clemency?" Mrs. Willis replies: "I am a practical woman of the world and I think your young woman builded wiser than she knew. I am of the opinion that most men are like the lower animals in many things—they don't always know what is for their best good." Mrs. Willis's advice does not sanction the father's law; instead, she insists that man's view is finite, while God's judgment is infinite. She interprets God's infinity as "[Sappho's] duty . . . to be happy and bright for the good of those about [her]." The preeminence of the mother's law also directs the lives of Will Smith and his sister, Dora. For them their father is a sacred memory, connecting them to a history of racial strength as well as oppression. However, his absence also mitigates the strength of patriarchal values on their immediate lives and permits their mother to become the authority figure who not only nurtures them but manages the household affairs. Although the text makes no explicit mention of her managerial skills, it informs us that she runs a comfortable rooming house, and has a son enrolled at Harvard and a daughter who does not work outside the home. These details represent Mrs. Smith's proficiency in financial management and encourages the characters ⟨and us⟩ to regard women not as masculine complements but as individuals in their own right, deserving respect. Equally important to the evolving plot, the absence of the father and his law permits Will to follow his own desire in selecting his wife, rather than institutionalized patriarchal desire for premarital virginity. As a result he is free to marry the so-called ruined woman and to father her child as if it were his own.

The fact that Mrs. Willis is also a widow is important because she and Mrs. Smith are the principal means for inscribing the absence of the black patriarch. Mrs. Smith is the ideal maternal figure, which the text underscores by repeatedly referring to her as Ma Smith. Her widowhood is idealized, while Mrs. Willis's widowhood is problematic. The text describes Mrs. Willis's deceased husband as "a bright Negro politician" who had secured "a seat in the Legislature." In addition, she had "loved [him] with a love ambitious for his advancement." Despite "the always expected addition to [their] family," she was the woman behind the man. However, at his death there was no trust fund to meet her financial needs, and she has to work. For her the question becomes what line of work can fulfill both her financial needs and ambition. No longer able to represent her ambition as desire for her husband's advancement, Mrs. Willis has to find a cause. "The best opening, she decided after looking carefully about her, was in the great cause of the evolution of true womanhood in the work of the 'Woman Question' as embodied in marriage and suffrage." Thus, Mrs. Willis comes to the Woman Question not out of a burning passion for women's rights but out of a desire to advance herself as well as black women and the race. In short, she is a professional, or, in her own words, "a practical woman of the world" who has "succeeded well in her plans," which the text continues to describe as "conceived in selfishness, they yet bore glorious fruit in the formation of clubs of colored women banded together . . . [to] better the condition of mankind." To her audience she is a "brilliant widow" who "could talk dashingly on many themes." However, Mrs. Willis incites "a wave of repulsion" in Sappho; yet "Sappho [is] impressed in spite of herself, by the woman's words." Mrs. Willis is a model for the successful professional woman of that epoch who has stepped far into the public realm of political ambition. Sappho detects Mrs. Willis's conscious desire for power as well as the will to grasp it, and this detection excites her contradictory feelings about women's ambitions for power and conventional gender prescriptives designating it as inappropriate, which Hopkins's contemporaries no doubt also experienced.

Claudia Tate, "Allegories of Black Female Desire; or, Rereading Nineteenth-Century Sentimental Narratives of Black Female Authority," *Changing Our Own Words: Essays on Criticism, Theory, and Writing by Black Women*, ed. Cheryl A. Wall (New Brunswick, NJ: Rutgers University Press, 1989), pp. 122–23.

ELIZABETH AMMONS   Very far removed from the social-documentary style of *Contending Forces*, *Of One Blood* mixes in unstable and therefore highly productive and unsettling combinations the ingredients of narrative realism, travelog, allegory, and dream prophecy. Unlike ⟨Frances E. W.⟩ Harper's work, in which much the same mixing of forms suggests generic searching, Hopkins's fusion, confusion, and irresolution of genre—the strange complexity of *Of One Blood*'s "fantastical plot," to recall Watson's characterization—suggests brilliant, even if not totally realized, purpose. Hopkins is not entering herself in the American romance tradition. She does not, like Hawthorne, use the supernatural as symbol. Rather, like Toni Morrison after her, she asserts the supernatural as reality. She breaks boundaries—enters the secret, long lost kingdom of black power in Africa—not in a mind trip but in a *real* trip, as *Of One Blood*'s literal volatility of

form expresses. She moves with complete logic and ease between material
and supernatural reality, past and present. In Charlotte Perkins Gilman's
work about a woman artist, spirits and the supernatural are products of
mind—and of deranged mind at that (the wobbling heads in the wallpaper,
the creeping female forms). In Hopkins's narrative, experience from the
other side (of life/of the world) is not the product of mind, much less of
insanity. It is part of what is here. To "say" this in fiction—to say the
opposite of what a Poe or Gilman might imply in their contextualizing of
the supernatural in madness, or what Hawthorne might suggest in using
the supernatural as moral or psychological symbol—Hopkins *does* create,
by "realistic" high-culture western standards, a most strange and fantastical
narrative: elaborate, dense, utterly decentered in its instability as realism.
Clearly her last published long fiction, *Of One Blood*, suggests her desire to
break out of the inherited high western narrative tradition, her desire to
craft new form by drawing on antidominant realities of multiconsciousness
and pan-African wholeness.

As an allegory about art, Hopkins's elaborate, bitter story shows the black
woman artist, whose roots go deep into African history, half-dead and then
completely dead in the United States. Dianthe, Candace's spiritual double
and daughter, should be strong like her African forbear: regal, powerful,
constantly renewed by the society in which she lives, and ready to unite
with the black man to redeem the past and create the future. In Hopkins's
myth, however, this tremendous possibility for creativity, including union
with her black brother, meets total destruction at the hands of the white
man, whose policy it is to deceive, silence, exploit sexually, and finally kill
the black woman if she attempts to free herself from him. Whatever guarded
optimism Hopkins might have felt about the future of the African American
woman artist at the time she wrote *Contending Forces* was gone by the time
she wrote *Of One Blood*. Grounding the black woman artist's story in
unrequited heterosexual desire, violent sexual violation by white America,
and erasure of her empowering African heritage, Hopkins tells in her "fairy
tale," her wildly unbelievable fiction (if looked at in conventional western
realistic terms), the awful truth about the African American woman artist's
reality at the beginning of the twentieth century. In *Of One Blood* the black
American woman artist *has* a past. It is ancient, potent, brilliant—full of
voice. What she does not have is ownership of that past, or a future. ⟨. . .⟩

With *Of One Blood* Pauline Hopkins changed history. She pushed narrative form fully over into the mode of allegorical vision, prophecy, and
dream projection that African American fiction, and particularly fiction by
women—Toni Morrison, Rosa Guy, Gloria Naylor—would brilliantly mine

later in the twentieth century. Without the *Colored American Magazine*, however, Pauline Hopkins, whose last major fiction in that magazine dramatized the violent silencing and death of the black American woman artist, disappeared as a productive artist.

Elizabeth Ammons, "The Limits of Freedom: The Fiction of Alice Dunbar-Nelson, Kate Chopin, and Pauline Hopkins," *Conflicting Stories: American Women Writers at the Turn into the Twentieth Century* (New York: Oxford University Press, 1991), pp. 83–85

Bibliography

Contending Forces: A Romance Illustrative of Negro Life North and South. 1900.

A Primer of Facts Pertaining to the Greatness of the African Race and the Possibility of Restoration by Its Descendants. 1905.

Magazine Novels: Hagar's Daughter; Winona; Of One Blood. Ed. Hazel V. Carby. 1988.

Peculiar Sam; or, The Underground Railroad. n.d.

James Weldon Johnson
1871–1938

NEITHER OF JAMES WELDON JOHNSON'S parents had been slaves before the Civil War. His father, James, was born free in Virginia in 1830; his mother Helen Duttel was part Haitian, part French, and a member of the Bahamian black middle class. James William ("James Weldon" after 1913) was born on June 17, 1871, in Jacksonville, Florida, after his family escaped the economic depression in Nassau at that time.

In Florida, James, Sr., provided his family with a middle-class life accessible to only a small minority of blacks in the South of the late 1800s. As a teenager, Johnson visited New York and became fascinated with city life. At seventeen he worked as a secretary to a white physician and research scientist, Thomas Osgood Summers, whose character greatly influenced him. Summers saw Johnson as a social equal, encouraging the young man to read and write poetry.

At Atlanta University, modeled after Yale, Johnson received a classical education and wished to pursue public service; he was often an active participant in formal debates on the issue of race. Upon graduation, and after a stint as a principal, Johnson established the first high school for blacks, as well as creating America's first black daily newspaper, the Jacksonville *Daily American*. Upon its financial collapse, Johnson studied law and in 1896 was admitted to the Florida bar.

Johnson practiced law for part of the year but traveled to New York in the summer months to work with his brother, John Rosamund, and other black performers bound for Broadway and Europe. The Johnson brothers employed popular black imagery but avoided standard racist vocabulary. One of the earliest songs composed by the Johnsons, "Lift Every Voice and Sing," was composed for an Abraham Lincoln birthday celebration in 1900; this song was later adopted by the NAACP as their official song.

Johnson, in his early dialect poems and lyrics, drew upon a genre full of racial stereotypes, but he also accepted the reality of that dialect as an authentic language. He wished to reveal the deeper themes of history and the emotions of black Americans; yet he, and his critics as well, found the use of dialect problematic at best; even today it continues to be a topic for debate.

In 1906 Johnson entered foreign service as a U.S. consul in Venezuela and wrote his only work of fiction, *The Autobiography of an Ex-Colored Man* (published anonymously in 1912), a story modeled on an autobiographical narrative. After publishing his first book of poems, *Fifty Years and Other Poems* (1917), Johnson became Secretary of the NAACP and led a battle for a federal antilynching law, using his talents as a lawyer, public speaker, and lobbyist. Johnson was perhaps the leading proponent of black American culture in the 1920s. However, he became increasingly at odds with other black leaders and rejected communism, separatism, and violence as alternatives in the struggle for racial equality.

In 1930 Johnson published *Black Manhattan*, a still valuable study of black theatre in New York. His autobiography, *Along This Way*, followed in 1933. The last books to appear in his lifetime were the trenchant essay *Negro Americans, What Now?* (1934), and a selection of his poetry, *Saint Peter Relates an Incident* (1935).

Johnson died a sudden death when, on his sixty-seventh birthday (June 17, 1938), his automobile collided with a train while he was vacationing in Maine. He is buried in Greenwood Cemetery in Brooklyn, New York.

◈ Critical Extracts

SHERMAN, FRENCH & COMPANY   This vivid and startlingly new picture of conditions brought about by the race question in the United States makes no special plea for the Negro, but shows in a dispassionate, though sympathetic, manner conditions as they actually exist between the whites and blacks to-day. Special pleas have already been made for and against the Negro in hundreds of books, but in these books either his virtues or his vices have been exaggerated. This is because writers, in nearly every instance, have treated the colored American as a *whole*; each has taken some one group of the race to prove his case. Not before has a composite and proportionate presentation of the entire race, embracing all of its various groups and elements, showing their relations with each other and to the whites, been made.

It is very likely that the Negroes of the United States have a fairly correct idea of what the white people of the country think of them, for that opinion has for a long time been and is still being constantly stated; but they are themselves more or less a sphinx to the whites. It is curiously interesting and even vitally important to know what are the thoughts of ten millions of them concerning the people among whom they live. In these pages it is as though a veil had been drawn aside: the reader is given a view of the inner life of the Negro in America, is initiated into the "freemasonry," as it were, of the race.

These pages also reveal the unsuspected fact that prejudice against the Negro is exerting a pressure which, in New York and other large cities where the opportunity is open, is actually and constantly forcing an unascertainable number of fair-complexioned colored people over into the white race.

In this book the reader is given a glimpse behind the scenes of this race-drama which is being here enacted,—he is taken upon an elevation where he can catch a bird's-eye view of the conflict which is being waged.

Sherman, French & Company, "Preface," *The Autobiography of an Ex-Colored Man* by James Weldon Johnson (1912; rpt. New York: Penguin Books, 1990), pp. xxxiii–xxxiv

---

BENJAMIN BRAWLEY   Mr. Johnson's first formal publication, *Autobiography of an Ex-Colored Man*, was published anonymously in 1912, but in 1927 was given new issue with the author's name. The method of the book is primarily that of fiction, but the writer draws upon his own experiences as freely as he chooses. So doing he is able to interpret without any restriction the life of which he has been a part. In the career of the central figure who, born in Georgia, attends school in Connecticut, and later looks large-eyed upon the world, the book touches upon practically every phase of the so-called Negro problem. While it is as fresh to-day as when it was written, it shows clearly that it anticipated the hectic temper that we have had in Negro literature and music since the war. At the close the character of whom we have spoken has decided, after many misgivings, to remain beyond the color-line. He is not satisfied, however. He attends a meeting in Carnegie Hall, hears Booker T. Washington speak and the Hampton students sing, and he feels that he too, had he not been small and selfish, might have made his life great, and been part of the glorious work of making a race.

Benjamin Brawley, *The Negro in Literature and Art in the United States* (New York: Duffield & Co., 1921), pp. 100–101

DAVID LITTLEJOHN   J. W. Johnson's *The Autobiography of an Ex-Colored Man* (1912) is more a social phenomenon than a novel, and its notoriety—some of which has endured—is the combined product of its once-daring title, its anonymous publication (which led readers to presume it factual for fifteen years), and the novelty of its "outspoken" message to 1912 America. It reveals itself today as an utterly artless, unstructured, unselective sequence of Negro-life episodes, written in a style as flat and directionless as the floor of an enormous room. The climactic episodes, moreover—the hero's high life in Bohemian New York as a ragtime pianist, his European tour with a millionaire patron—betray only adolescent fantasies beneath the dull surface of prose. More interesting is what Johnson reveals, of America and himself, between the lines of plot. His essayette digressions, for example, offer a fair view of the antediluvian race relations in America during this period, albeit a view peculiarly fogged by his own prejudices: W. E. B. DuBois is a far more dependable authority. The prejudices themselves, though, the self-revelation, may have for some white readers still a strangely pathetic appeal. He—the "hero," if not Johnson—is a pure example of the self-styled "better class of Negroes," a member of DuBois' "Talented Tenth," who hoped in these distant, deluded years to effect a liaison with "the better class of whites," and to detach himself utterly from the despised lower Negro classes.

> The unkempt appearance, the shambling slouching gait and loud talk and laughter of these people aroused in me a feeling of almost repulsion.
> . . . odd as it may sound, refined coloured people get no more pleasure out of riding with offensive Negroes than anybody else would get. . . .
> Happily, this class represents the black people of the South far below their normal physical and moral condition, but in its increase lies the possibility of grave dangers. . . .
> I can imagine no more dissatisfied being than an educated, cultured, and refined coloured man in the United States.

Along with this class consciousness goes a dilettantish championing of the popular Negro arts, reminiscent of the detached folklorist's interest one feels in *God's Trombones*. His hero lists, in fact, the Uncle Remus stories, the Jubilee songs, ragtime, and the cake-walk as the four great cultural contributions of the American Negro, and paragraphs of his prose are devoted to the latter two. *The Autobiography* is anything but a "good" book; but, for all the naïveté, the snobbery, the fantasy, and the flatness, it does afford a unique and perhaps useful portrait of a period and a type.

David Littlejohn, *Black on White: A Critical Survey of Writing by American Negroes* (New York: Grossman, 1966), pp. 26–27

EUGENE LEVY   Like many creative writers, Johnson felt that art and social criticism were fundamentally different forms of expression, though each might be of use to the other. Art could not be produced for the purpose of propaganda. Art such as Forster's *A Passage to India* or the singing of Ethel Waters, however, in certain subtle ways could expand our understanding of a social problem like racism. Writers such as McKay and Hughes, Johnson believed, demonstrated to the American public that black men could create valid art by drawing for their material upon a significant social phenomenon—the life of the Afro-American. Johnson saw this as contributing to the breakdown of racial separation in American society, thus pushing society closer to his goal of integration.

For those who believed that goal to be both invalid and unrealizable, however, men like Hughes, McKay, and Johnson were simply deceiving blacks when they claimed that demonstrating one's ability would bring opportunity. Perhaps the most outspoken advocate in the 1920s of this viewpoint was Marcus Garvey, a man with few friends among intellectuals, either black or white. Garvey did nothing to conceal the profound distrust he felt toward whites, or toward blacks who tried to convince whites they ought to share the wealth and power of Euro-America with its black population. W. E. B. Du Bois, one of Garvey's most vitriolic critics, nevertheless shared with the Back to Africa leader a profound skepticism toward putting faith in whites. The white power structure, at least as it existed in the United States in the 1920s, seemed unlikely to be converted to brotherhood by the artistry of Ethel Waters or the insight of Gertrude Stein. Along with the sexual prudery of his views toward the Renaissance, Du Bois firmly believed that only the fist of hard-hitting propaganda, not the velvet glove of art, would stop the oppression of white over black.

On one matter Garvey, Du Bois, Johnson, and the writers of the Renaissance agreed: the necessity of pride in the race's past and present accomplishments. Booker T. Washington expressed it for them when he wrote: "It was with a race as it is with an individual: it must respect itself if it would win the respect of others." Johnson, along with most of the younger writers, however, was far more optimistic than Garvey or Du Bois as to the influence black writers might have on American society. He had his differences with the younger writers, largely stemming from his attachment to what was essentially a modified "melting pot" conception of America's future. Blacks should further develop their own culture so as to establish themselves in American society, but, once that had been accomplished, it would be wisest and safest, Johnson had maintained for many years, to meld into a fully unified national culture. Black writers such as Locke, Hughes, and Countee Cullen, on the other hand, put much more emphasis on maintaining a unique black culture. They adhered to a "nation of nations" conception: black Americans, like Euro-American ethnic groups, would develop their own hyphenated culture, but all Americans would cooperate in maintaining an equitable and productive society. Such differences in ends were theoretical in the social situation of the 1920s. Those of the Renaissance agreed on means, and especially on the role of art in race progress and reconciliation. After reading *The Autobiography of an Ex-Colored Man*, Aaron Douglas— the black artist who illustrated many of the books of the Renaissance, including *God's Trombones*—wrote Johnson: "The post-war Negro, blinded by the glare and almost sudden bursting of a new day, finds much difficulty in realizing the immense power and effort . . . the pre-war Negro . . . made to prepare the country for what we now feel to be the new awakening." The "new awakening," of course, awoke fewer than Douglas, in his enthusiasm, seemed to think—a fact many black writers were to learn in the 1930s. Nevertheless, the sense of change as well as of continuity with the past which he expressed in his letter reflected both a feeling and a reality which Johnson had done much to foster.

Eugene Levy, *James Weldon Johnson: Black Leader, Black Voice* (Chicago: University of Chicago Press, 1973), pp. 219–21

ARTHUR P. DAVIS   Johnson's full-length autobiography, *Along This Way* (1930), adopts the pattern of Negro autobiography of the age: a combination of middle-class success story, racial vindication, and social commentary, rather than "pure" delineation of personality. The work, however, is valuable because Johnson had such a varied and outstanding career and knew so many prominent persons, white and black, of his age. The most fascinating parts are not the ones connected with the Dyer Anti-Lynching Bill and other important political matters, but rather those dealing with the vignettes that crop up: Paul Laurence Dunbar's reaction to the poetry of Walt Whitman, midnight parties with black celebrities at the old Marshall Hotel, contacts with Broadway characters such as Flo Ziegfeld and Anna Held, and, above all, Black Bohemia in the 53rd Street area. One enjoys reading *Along This Way*, yet leaves it with a feeling that this success story is too successful, too upward looking; it is all peaks with few or no pits of failure and ugliness. The reason, perhaps, is the best-foot-foremost philosophy that motivated Johnson's generation. Determined to prove to white America that they could make the grade, these writers became automatic salesmen, selling the Talented Tenth to the nation, although by 1935 they would not have used the phrase. What *Along This Way* really says is this: See what I have done in spite of the pressures you put on me. I am like you—the best of you, of course; so count me in.

Black Manhattan has a twofold purpose: it gives .he history of the Negro in New York, emphasizing his presence in Harlem; it also gives a very useful account of the Negro in the theatre from 1821, the time of the African Company, to 1930, the year in which *Green Pastures* played on Broadway. *Black Manhattan* is a very useful source book for those who write on the black theatre. It has sketches of many famous performers of yesteryear, accounts of the first attempts of Negroes to form theatre companies; a record of failures and achievements in the theatre—all written by a man who was himself part of that theatre world, part of that Black Bohemia about which he writes. Needless to say, some of the material in *Black Manhattan* is also found in Johnson's novel and autobiography. Coming out in 1930 in the dead center of the Harlem Renaissance, the work was timely. In the recent upsurge of interest in black life, the work is once more in demand. It has stood the test of time well.

Arthur P. Davis, "James Weldon Johnson," *From the Dark Tower: Afro-American Writers, 1900 to 1960* (Washington, DC: Howard University Press, 1974), pp. 31–32

ROBERT B. STEPTO   While *The Autobiography*'s indebtedness to antecedent texts (especially *Up from Slavery* and *The Souls of Black Folk*) tell us much about how Johnson fashioned "something new and unknown," they tell us only a partial story of his narrative's literary past. The rest of the story involves *The Autobiography*'s literary future, and especially its literary present. Only by discovering this literary present may we assume that the narrative achieves enough integrity to begin to predict a literary future. In this regard one feature of *The Autobiography* stands out from the rest: its uncompromising study of race and music in the world of Mammon. This feature constitutes a nearly sacrilegious inversion of those hallowed tropes in Afro-American art which remain responsible for the culture's abiding belief in the essential oneness of its music and tribal integrity. While it certainly can be argued that the feature is to some degree an indebtedness, since it inverts preexisting tropes found in the writings of Dunbar, Du Bois, and others, the quality of the inversion is such that the feature finally must be assigned to a new category, namely, that of "anticipation." In this particular instance, the distinction between an indebtedness and an anticipation is quite specifically that between a literary feature that inverts and one that demystifies a preexisting trope. To be sure, the line between these two activities can be quite fine, but that is part (and probably most) of the point: the line is fine because indebtedness and anticipations *both* exist in a given text's literary present.

I want to suggest here that *The Autobiography*'s demystification of the "sacred" bond between Afro-America's music and its tribal integrity is not only part of the "something new," creating fresh space for the narrative in Afro-American letters, but also a feature anticipating certain prominent tropes and expressions in the literature to come. Indeed, once the music is heard in Mammon's lair as well as in cultural ritual grounds such as the Black Belt, both the sacred and secular (if not exactly profane) strains in the music and the discrete subcultures enveloping each become artistic subjects, especially in periods such as those following the publication of *The Autobiography*, when there is an interst in a literary social realism. While it can be argued that Johnson "broke the new wood" for subsequent Afro-American (and American) literary ventures, it also can be said that he almost singlehandedly created a great deal of havoc. When Afro-American literary critics in the 1920's (including especially Du Bois) roundly condemned those vivid portraits of Negro America's urban underbelly in the "renaissance" writings of Claude McKay, Langston Hughes, and others, they sustained, albeit from their own point of view, a peculiarly American notion of degeneracy and sordidness which achieves its greatest frenzy in the face of spatial configurations of music, interracial liaison, and intemperance such as the Negro cabaret. In *The Autobiography* the Club where the Ex-Coloured Man is first introduced to ragtime music and "coloured Bohemia," as well as to his future patron and "the rich widow," inaugurates all such spatial configurations in modern Afro-American letters. It does so because it is not so much a setting as a symbolic space.

The significance of Johnson's invention becomes clear when we not only look forward in literary history to the literature fashioned by Jean Toomer, Langston Hughes, Claude McKay, and Sterling Brown, but also turn back once again to texts by Du Bois and Washington. *The Souls of Black Folk* and *Up from Slavery* are seminal texts in Afro-American letters partly because each contributes to the series of symbolic spaces in the tradition. In the case of the former, there is first and foremost the Black Belt, but also the consummate construction of Du Bois's Atlanta study; in the latter, the chief symbolic space is Tuskegee itself. Coming hard upon the heels of these volumes, *The Autobiography*'s novel and in many ways abrasive assertion is that the Ex-Coloured Man's Club, in all its external and internal complexities, is a compact world unto itself, a world of no less significance and resonance in Afro-American art and life than that readily assigned to Du Bois's and Washington's more agreeable constructions.

Robert B. Stepto, "Lost in a Quest: James Weldon Johnson's *The Autobiography of an Ex-Coloured Man*," *From Behind the Veil: A Study of Afro-American Narrative* (Urbana: University of Illinois Press, 1979), pp. 121–23

CHIDI IKONNÉ   It is true that some of the narrator's utterances in *Autobiography* reveal elements of contempt for black people. His reaction to the black population of Atlanta is a case in point. "The unkempt appearance, the shambling, slouching gait and loud talk and laughter of these people aroused in me a feeling of almost repulsion." Yet it must be remembered that he has been brought up as "a perfect little aristocrat." He could have reacted in the same way to a white population of the same class. In other words, the repulsion he feels stems more from class consciousness than from an awareness of the color of his skin.

His motivation and experience are so lifelike that when the novel first appeared in 1912, many people believed that it was a true story. Even as late as 1932 Arthur Ficke apparently still identified James Weldon Johnson with his narrator. This attempt to present a Negro element as he really is, without any falsification to please or hurt anyone, is ⟨. . .⟩ a feature of the Harlem Renaissance literature.

The pride implicit in it, and in the treatment which folkways receive in the novel is another tribute to the growing self-confidence from which black literature of the 1920s would derive its daredevil self-assertiveness. Notice, for instance, the self-confident pride implicit in the narrator's projection of Uncle Remus stories, the jubilee songs, the ragtime music, and the cakewalk as some of the Negro's greatest gifts to America. With particular reference to ragtime he asserts: "No one who has travelled can question the world-conquering influence of ragtime, and I do not think it would be an exaggeration to say that in Europe the United States is popularly known by rag-time than by anything else it has produced in a generation."

It is the same self-confidence that underlies the depiction of the Negro folk religion in the "big meeting" sequence as well as the unbashful, unapologetic portrayal of the goings-on at the "Club." The self-confidence is also evident in the discussion of the Negro dialect and folk humor, even though that discussion is tinged with condescension—a condescension which, in any case, is understandable since the narrator, who is also the main actor, is very much above the standard of living of the people with whom he is dealing.

Chidi Ikonné, *From Du Bois to Van Vechten: The Early New Negro Literature, 1903–1926* (Westport, CT: Greenwood Press, 1981), pp. 69–70

LADELL PAYNE   Johnson's "I" (in *The Autobiography of an Ex-Colored Man*) was born in Georgia shortly after the Civil War. Rather than telling the reader that his narrator is black, Johnson has him recall impressions of the house, the flowers, the glass-bottle hedge, the wash tubs, the vegetable garden which surrounded him, the bread and molasses which he ate. In short, he remembers details which tell us that he almost certainly came from a southern rural Negro home. He also remembers the tall man with the shiny boots, the gold chain, and the watch, who visited his mother from time to time and who hung a ten dollar gold piece with a hole drilled in it around his neck as a gift when the narrator and his mother moved north to Connecticut. In Connecticut the narrator demonstrates some musical talent and is given piano lessons. He is also a good student. He is splendidly happy until one day, when he is about ten years old, his teacher identifies him as a Negro before the class. Like many other southern protagonists, black and white, he is shattered by a knowledge he cannot comprehend. In Faulkner's *Absalom, Absalom!* (1936), Mr. Compson imagines Charles Etienne de Saint Velery Bon, when he is told "that he was, must be, a negro," looking at himself in "the shard of broken mirror" during "what hours of amazed and tearless grief . . . examining himself . . . with quiet and incredulous incomprehension." In Johnson's 1912 novel, the protagonist rushes to his room and goes quickly to his looking glass.

> For an instant I was afraid to look, but when I did, I looked long
> and earnestly. . . . I was accustomed to hear remarks about
> my beauty; but now, for the first time, I became conscious of it
> and recognized it. I noticed the ivory whiteness of my skin,
> the beauty of my mouth, the size and liquid darkness of my
> eyes. . . . I noticed the softness and glossiness of my dark
> hair. . . . How long I stood there gazing at my image I do not
> know. . . . I ran downstairs and rushed to where my mother
> was sitting. . . . I buried my head in her lap and blurted out:
> "Mother, mother, tell me, am I a nigger?"

He is, in effect, asking his mother who he is. She answers that he is neither a "nigger" nor white; her refusal even to name his father makes his identity even more equivocal. Nameless, raceless, fatherless, like the Joe Christmas of Faulkner's *Light in August*, he is a person without a definable self. And also like Christmas, he assumes a racial identity based, as Cleanth Brooks has pointed out, on a state of mind rather than on the possession of Negro genes: "And so I have often lived through that hour, that day, that week, in which was wrought the miracle of my transition from one world into another; for I did indeed pass into another world. From that time I looked out through other eyes, my thoughts were coloured, my words dictated, my actions limited by one dominating, all-pervading idea which constantly increased in force and weight until I finally realized in it a great, tangible fact."

Ladell Payne, "Themes and Cadences: James Weldon Johnson, 1871–1938." *Black Novelists and the Southern Literary Tradition* (Athens: University of Georgia Press, 1981), pp. 28–29

HOWARD FAULKNER   What I want to argue is that *The Autobiography* is the first black novel to be totally of a piece: a small masterpiece of control. What critics have faulted is not truly digression or artlessness. Rather, the insipid style and the apparent lack of purposeful selectivity are a direct expression of the narrator's character and of his inability to feel deeply what is happening to him and to put those events in perspective; similarly, the discussion and analysis of black life and people are not adventitious nor are they intrusions of Johnson's own beliefs, but further revelations of character. Our reaction is more problematic than it would be were the irony less subtle, for the narrator is an educated, articulate, and sensitive hero, or anti-hero, and we are thus likely to begin by giving his ideas credence. But we must never mistake the persona for Johnson or think that Johnson lets the ironic tone drop: He does not, in his life story of a man who finally realizes that he has had no life to report.

It is a novel to set beside such other small works of "the unlived life" as Henry James' "The Beast in the Jungle," F. Scott Fitzgerald's "The Rich Boy," and Saul Bellow's *Seize the Day*. In each of these novellas, as in *The Autobiography*, a protagonist of sufficient intelligence, means, and sophistication has a chance to make of his life something significant. Each work is structured around a series of events which involves a protagonist who fails to act or whose action may more accurately be defined as a withdrawal. Each story thus risks boredom; the "fallacy of imitative form" seems for

each author a real peril: how to portray boredom without becoming weari-
some. The protagonists have chance after chance to act, to learn, to be,
but fail over and over again, and the story must present this slow, willful,
and consistent failure in order for us to understand the texture of their
lives. Because the focus is consistently on one character and because that
character's lack of perception is the tonal key, the narrative style must have
about it a certain flatness. Finally, each story ends with the protagonist's
epiphany, his understanding that though he remains literally alive, his
chance to live meaningfully is behind him; ironically, though, the habits
of their lifetimes make the protagonists unable even to feel completely the
horror of that understanding. In each of the works, that epiphany follows
immediately the death of another character: James' protagonist learns after
the death of Mary Bartram, the woman who has loved him; Fitzgerald's learns
after the death of his first love, Paula Legendre. For Bellow's protagonist the
funeral he stumbles into is of a man he has not known, and yet his sorrow
rises like waves, engulfing him; and in *The Autobiography*, the protagonist
has just realized what he calls the second great sorrow of his life, the death
of his wife. ⟨. . .⟩

   The Autobiography of an Ex-Coloured Man is the first fully realized black
American novel, a beautiful story of the fear of never living, of being only
a detached observer of life. Johnson gives it the peculiar twist that the
birthright sold, the beast in the jungle that never springs, the day that is
never seized—all depend on the acceptance of blackness, of manhood, of
life with all its dangers and impurities. The ex-coloured man is the first
protagonist in black fiction to be destroyed from within. In his striving to
free himself from limitation, he is perfectly successful in effacing himself,
in reducing himself and his life to invisibility.

        Howard Faulkner, "James Weldon Johnson's Portrait of the Artist as Invisible Man,"
        Black American Literature Forum 19, No. 4 (Winter 1985): 148, 151

WILLIAM L. ANDREWS   James Weldon Johnson ⟨. . .⟩ realized
that real moral as well as literary advantages could be gained by allowing
a black character to turn inward and tell his own story, even if that story
involved confessions of the sort that might seem detrimental to the larger
interests of the race. The African-American narrative tradition, from the
earliest autobiographies of fugitive slaves to the most accomplished novels
of Chesnutt and Du Bois, had been inspired by a desire to testify to the
full humanity of black people, despite all the racist propaganda that white
America could muster. What better testimonial could be offered than that

of a black narrator bent on genuine self-reflection and candid self-criticism? Readers and critics of the *Autobiography* have questioned the extent to which the narrator of the novel really understands himself or his foibles and failings. It is nevertheless true that the ex-colored man is motivated by a desire to work out, through the act of autobiography, his complex and sometimes contradictory attitudes toward himself in order to arrive finally at some satisfying sense of his own identity. However the narrator of the *Autobiography* comes to define himself—racially, socially, intellectually, and morally—his story cannot be taken as anything less than "a human document," to use Johnson's phrase. The insight, judgment, taste, and honorableness of this narrator may be challenged, but not his humanity. The fact that so much has been argued and so little has been resolved about what motivates the narrator, what he means by many of his statements, and what Johnson intended him to signify only confirms the *Autobiography*'s inexhaustible appeal as a narrative that invokes, via an African-American's various crises of identity, the human drama of modernity in late nineteenth- and early twentieth-century America. ⟨. . .⟩

Ever since the *Autobiography* first appeared, there have been readers and reviewers of the book who have judged the narrator a failure at best, or a coward at worst, for severing all his ties to black America at the end of the novel. Yet in several places in his story the narrator offers various social and economic, as well as ethical, justifications for this kind of action. It seems unlikely that Johnson himself would have faulted the narrator in the abstract for opting to become, in effect, racially neutral, "neither disclaim[ing] the black race nor claim[ing] the white race," but simply "let[ting] the world take me for what it would." In *Along This Way*, Johnson professed his belief that ultimately racial differences in America would be amalgamated to the point where "the Negro will fuse his qualities with those of the other groups in the making of the ultimate American people." If whites are so concerned about race-mixing, Johnson's novel suggests, they ought to ensure a society of equal opportunities and rights for all Americans so that a person like the narrator of the *Autobiography* will not feel obliged to become an ex-colored man in order to have a fair chance for fulfillment.

William L. Andrews, "Introduction," *The Autobiography of an Ex-Colored Man* by James Weldon Johnson (New York: Penguin, 1990), pp. xviii–xix, xxv

Bibliography

The Autobiography of an Ex-Colored Man. 1912.

Fifty Years and Other Poems. 1917.

Self-Determining Haiti. 1920.

The Book of American Negro Poetry (editor). 1922, 1931.

The Book of Negro Spirituals (editor; with J. Rosamond Johnson). 1925.

The Second Book of American Negro Spirituals (editor; with J. Rosamond Johnson). 1926.

God's Trombones: Seven Negro Sermons in Verse. 1927.

Native African Races and Culture. 1927.

Saint Peter Relates an Incident of the Resurrection Day. 1930.

Black Manhattan. 1930.

The Shining Life: An Appreciation of Julius Rosenwald. 1932.

Along This Way: The Autobiography of James Weldon Johnson. 1933.

Negro Americans, What Now? 1934.

Saint Peter Relates an Incident: Selected Poems. 1935.

Oscar Micheaux
1884–1951

OSCAR MICHEAUX was born on January 2, 1884, on a farm near Metropolis, Illinois, the fifth of thirteen children of Calvin and Belle Willingham Michaux (the original spelling of the name). Although educated in schools in Metropolis, Micheaux was not satisfied with the insular life there and left at the age of seventeen. After holding a series of menial jobs, including porter on a Pullman car, he headed west, occupying a small homestead in Gregory County, South Dakota. It was this experience that led him to write his first work, *The Conquest: The Story of a Negro Pioneer* (1913), published anonymously as "By the Pioneer." This work is frequently assumed to be a novel, but—in spite of the fact that the protagonist's name is altered to Oscar Devereaux and other names are changed—it is in fact Micheaux's autobiography. The work is dedicated to Booker T. Washington, whose belief in the uplifting of the black race through hard work and self-discipline Micheaux had adopted.

Micheaux became his own salesman for *The Conquest,* traveling throughout South Dakota and then the South to sell copies of it. This enterprise proved so successful that Micheaux founded his own publishing company, the Western Book Supply, then based in Lincoln, Nebraska, and in 1915 issued his first true novel, *The Forged Note: A Romance of the Darker Races.* This work is also very autobiographical: it features a protagonist who is a homesteader in South Dakota and the author of a book of his experiences, and who then undertakes to sell copies of his book through the South. This framework allows Micheaux to focus on the problems of blacks in the South, problems Micheaux evidently believed to be largely self-caused because of a lack of moral strength on the part of blacks and the lack of a cohesive social structure that would allow blacks to assist each other.

Micheaux's next novel, *The Homesteader* (1917), also published by the Western Book Supply (now in Sioux City, Iowa), is a romance involving a love triangle between a black man, a white woman, and a black woman. The book, although melodramatic and with a contrived happy ending, interested the Lincoln Motion Picture Company, a firm devoted to producing films by blacks for black audiences. Micheaux could not come to terms with the company and boldly decided to film the book himself, although he had no experience in film. The film, appearing in 1922, was a relative success, and permitted Micheaux to form the Micheaux Book and Film Company.

For the next twenty years Micheaux abandoned writing and devoted himself to writing, producing, and directing films. He produced many silent films in the 1920s, including *The Homesteader* (1922), an adaptation of his own novel, and *Body and Soul* (1924), in which Paul Robeson made his screen debut. Micheaux's company went into bankruptcy in 1928 but was saved by the contributions of white financiers. In 1931 Micheaux produced the first all-black talkie, *The Exile*. Throughout his film career Micheaux faced criticism for the low production quality of his films and for the frequently negative depictions of blacks in them.

In the 1940s Micheaux decided to resume writing, but his later works were not successful. *The Wind from Nowhere* (1941) is a reworking of *The Conquest*; *The Case of Mrs. Wingate* (1944) is a thriller involving Nazi spies and a black detective; *The Story of Dorothy Stanfield* (1946) is a sensational novel about an insurance scam; and *The Masquerade* (1947) is a transparent reworking of Charles W. Chesnutt's *The House Behind the Cedars* (1900). Oscar Micheaux died on a book tour in Charlotte, North Carolina, on March 26, 1951.

▣ *Critical Extracts*

HOWARD A. PHELPS   The most popular author of the city is Oscar Micheaux, the author of *The Homesteader*. He supervised the motion picture production of that name and manages the Micheaux Book and Film Company at 8 South Dearborn street. When the play *The Homesteader* played to big crowds at the Eighth Regiment Armory the "know-alls" predicted it had run its course in Chicago. Quite to the contrary, it has filled fourteen other engagements on the South Side and the show houses are clamoring for its return. This is by far the best motion picture yet written, acted and staged by a Colored man. It deserves all the loyal support the race has given it.

Howard A. Phelps, "Negro Life in Chicago," *Half-Century Magazine* 6, No. 5 (May 1919): 14

HUGO M. GLOSTER   Though unimpressive in technique, Oscar Micheaux's novels introduce characters and settings far removed from the well-trod paths of American Negro fiction. The problem of intermarriage, the cardinal interest in *The Conquest* and *The Homesteader*, is left dangling in the former work but is solved in the latter through the hackneyed device of revealing that the supposedly white heroine is a mixed-blood. *The Conquest*, which attempts to defend the program of Booker T. Washington, proposes Negro migration to the Northwest as a means of improving race relations in the South. In *The Forged Note* the author missed an unusual opportunity to probe the life of the Southern urban Negro. With all their inadequacies, however, Micheaux's novels stand in contrast to much of the complementary fiction produced by many Negro writers before the World War.

Hugo M. Gloster, *Negro Voices in American Fiction* (Chapel Hill: University of North Carolina Press, 1948), pp. 88–89

DONALD BOGLE   Micheaux used the same techniques in promoting and financing his films that he had used with his books. But he had a new dash and flair, befitting a motion-picture director. A hefty six-footer, given to wearing long Russian coats and extravagant wide-brimmed hats, Micheaux is said to have toured the country, stepping out of cars and into meeting halls as if "he were God about to deliver a sermon." "Why, he was so impressive and so charming," said Lorenzo Tucker, one of the most important of Micheaux's leading men, "that he could talk the shirt off your back." Just this sort of charm enabled Micheaux to persuade Southern theater owners to show his films. On his tours, Micheaux approached white Southerners and told them of the new black audience. At first they shied away, but when he spoke of the cash register, theater managers listened. It was soon arranged to have Micheaux features shown at special matinee performances held for black audiences. His movies were also sometimes shown at midnight performances for white audiences eager for black camp. Aware of the mystique of black nightclubs, he inserted into his films cabaret scenes that would appeal to whites.

As for his actors, Micheaux generally gathered them from black acting companies such as the Lafayette Players in New York. But he came across some of his stars under bizarre circumstances. Legend has it that Micheaux would spot a figure or note a gesture or be struck by the way the light fell across a face and would immediately sign the person up. Lorenzo Tucker said he was first spotted by Micheaux in Philadelphia. Having gone there to audition for a show, he was sitting in the lobby of the Dunbar Hotel

when crafty Micheaux, whom he did not know, approached him and asked
if he was an actor. "You're one of them who *thinks* they are," Micheaux
added. Afterward, Tucker went to see Micheaux in New York. He was given
a part, and all in all worked in some fourteen Micheaux productions.

Micheaux cast his actors on the basis of type. He modeled his stars
after white Hollywood personalities and publicized them as black versions.
Handsome and smooth Lorenzo Tucker was first referred to as the "black
Valentino." Later when talkies came in, he was the "colored William Pow-
ell." Sexy and insolent Bee Freeman, a vamp figure, was the "sepia Mae
West." Slick Chester, a character actor who played gangster roles, was the
"colored Cagney." Lovely Ethel Moses was sometimes touted as the "Negro
Harlow." The leads in Micheaux pictures were usually played by light-
colored Negro actors, and in later years Micheaux was to be severely criticized
by more militant black audiences for selecting "light-brights."

Once Micheaux had completed a film, he carried stills from it to theater
managers. "Here's my black Valentino. The girls love him," he would boast.
"If I can get the right backing, I'll star him in my next film, too." In this
way he was often able to solicit financing for his *next* picture. He also sent
his stars on personal-appearance junkets to Northern ghetto theaters. By
these vigorous promotion tactics he established himself as the most successful
black moviemaker of the period.

Donald Bogle, *Toms, Coons, Mulattoes, Mammies, and Bucks: An Interpretive History
of Blacks in American Films* (New York: Continuum, 1973 [rev. ed. 1989]), pp. 111–14

DANIEL J. LEAB   Micheaux initially received high praise from the
black press for his endeavors and his enterprise ⟨in filmmaking⟩. But in time
critics began to take him to task for his depiction of the life of the black
community. As early as 1920 Lester Walton, though he praised a Micheaux
movie called *The Brute* (starring the black prizefighter Sam Langford), com-
mented at length on the scenes of crap games, black dives, wife-beating,
and women congregating to gamble. These scenes, Wilcox said, were "not
any too pleasing to those of us who desire to see the better side of Negro
life portrayed"; they reminded him of "the attitude of the daily press, which
magnifies our vices and minimizes our virtues." In 1925 Sylvester Russell
of the Pittsburgh *Courier* reported on his arguments with Micheaux about
"the objectionable race features" in the producer's films. Other black newspapers also criticized Micheaux, but seemingly their objections made little
impression on him.

Although Micheaux could and did ignore his critics in the black press, he could not disregard his film company's deteriorating financial condition. The return on even the most successful black film was relatively small. There were about 20,000 movie theaters in the United States in 1926, but only a few hundred of these would play an all-black production, and theaters that catered to ghetto audiences charged reduced admission prices. Even if one includes the Southern theaters that had special midnight showings for blacks, the potential earnings were severely limited. And rarely did a black producer reach all the possible exhibitors, given his necessarily makeshift system of distribution. Micheaux was a clever businessman, but he was no exception.

Moreover, the novelty of the all-black movie was beginning to wear thin. In 1917 the New York *Age*, although acknowledging the drawbacks of a Douglass company movie, still praised it as "a racial business venture which ought to be encouraged." But, already by 1920 the *Age* was pointing out that "the day of expecting charitable consideration in business even of our own people just because we are Negroes is past." Though Micheaux's films did improve technically, they still remained amateurish by comparison with Hollywood's products. Ghetto audiences began to stay away from "race productions," and as one black newspaperman noted, "the worst enemy of the race production is the race movie fan himself." In February 1928, the Micheaux Film Corporation filed a voluntary petition of bankruptcy. It should be noted that Micheaux, ever the careful businessman, had seen to it that most of the corporation's films were legally the property of his wife.

Oscar Micheaux's silent motion picture works cannot be considered outstanding. He is significant, however, because he was one of the first independent black producers making popular and for a time profitable movies with black actors and actresses for ghetto audiences. Despite his public utterances, Micheaux's films were not designed to uplift or to enlighten. They were meant to entertain, to appeal to his concept of black popular taste, and to make money.

> Daniel J. Leab, *From Sambo to Superspade: The Black Experience in Motion Pictures* (Boston: Houghton Mifflin, 1975), pp. 79–81

ARLENE ELDER   Micheaux's story of his life on the South Dakota Prairie is doubly significant. First, it represents an American ideal at the turn of the century—the movement west and the opening up of the country. More interesting for the student of cultural pluralism, however, is Micheaux's self-conscious emotional division between personal ambition, marked by intense frontier individualism, and his hope of being not only a racial representative but a leader of his people and a model for them. Reflective of this paradoxical self-image is the contrast he establishes between the City and the Wilderness as he develops his theme of the West. This symbolic juxtaposition also serves as the organizing principle for his discussion of race.

Like the writings of other regionalists, Micheaux's books provide a wealth of topographical, historical, and political information. He gives details about the methods of holding lotteries to settle the country (first choice of a homesite going to the holder of the first number pulled from a pile by a blindfolded child); the astonishing way new towns sprang up almost overnight on the prairie; and the way two-story buildings in the town which boomed a few months before would be sawn in half and both parts moved to the next settlement boosted by the local businessmen, who had themselves started from nothing and flourished overnight. He enlightens us on the condition of the Indians, especially the social history of families of "breeds" like the Amoureaux who were ranchers, owners of great herds of cattle and much land, and "high moguls in little Crow society." He emphasizes the importance of the railroad in making or breaking the fortunes of the towns and farms in its path; and he skillfully describes the appearance and unusual features of the new country, frequently described as "the hollow of God's hand." Despite Micheaux's interest in local color, however, his real subject is himself. The introduction to his autobiography ⟨The Conquest⟩ states: "This is a true story of a negro who was discontented and the circumstances that were the outcome of that discontent."

Arlene Elder, "Oscar Micheaux: The Melting Pot on the Plains," *Old Northwest* 2, No. 3 (September 1976): 299–300

THOMAS CRIPPS   Nearly all of Micheaux's films are lost. If one of the silent pictures must stand for his canon it would be *Body and Soul* (1924), both for what it said and for the response it evoked. The picture represented the highest level of achievement for Micheaux. For the first time he wrestled with the nature of the black community, without recourse to shoddy devices, overdressing in the good cloth of Dunbar or Chesnutt, or interracial sensationalism. The theme allowed full play to his racial consciousness. To his stable of new stars he added Paul Robeson, fresh from triumphs on the white man's stage and football fields at Rutgers. The result was a rich black imagery that never materialized in other survivals of the 1920s and a modest accommodation with black intellectuals. For years black leaders, including Booker T. Washington, had railed against "jackleg" preachers who exploited the deep religiosity of poor blacks who settled in cold ghettos and turned to the charismatic churches as visible proof that their old Southern rural lives still had meaning. In *Body and Soul* Micheaux not only exposed cultist parasites but also advertised the promise that blacks could organize against the bootleggers and gamblers in their midst.

Not that Micheaux worked out all the themes in lonely isolation. To the contrary, his first print submitted to the New York censor board presented the preacher as the embodiment of unredeemed evil, with not a single redemptive quality in the black community. The New York censors would not tolerate it for much the same reason the NAACP would have given. So Micheaux recut it and fabricated an elaborate and confusing sequence which allowed the ingenue to awake and find that the preacher was a covert spy assigned to break up a bootlegging ring. If blacks could make movies in isolation, they still could not release them until white eyes had approved them. Furthermore, whites seemed to have developed a sensitivity to racial slurs that escaped the cavalier Micheaux.

The second version, bearing white fingermarks, may have given rounded dimensions to Negro life. The balance demanded by the censor board broadened the scope of the conflict and forced the characters into protagonist-antagonist tension. In the case of Paul Robeson's preacher, it enlarged the role into complex parts. In a dual role he brought power to the gambler's cynical smile and to the preacher's practical piety. Micheaux gave him tight closeups that tilted up to capture a virility long missing from black figures. Robeson fairly oozed the strength and sexuality of enthusiastic religion while at the same time giving off the hard, ominous energy of the "bad nigger" gambler. For Robeson, it was one of the few occasions when he cut free of white direction and bridged the deep fissure in the black world between the venal, erotic Staggerlee and respectable black bourgeois. His power carried him above the necessarily confused plot and allowed him to make a sensitive measurement of black character in American life.

Micheaux too reached high. In spite of the stagey, unmatched cutaway shots inherent in low-budget shooting, the garbled plot, and the broad comedy relief, he pulled off a modestly successful black movie. The exteriors had the rough and unpainted texture of Auburn Avenue, Beale Street, or some other black Southern promenade. The sets reinforced the dichotomy of the roles with simplistic, yet effective tricks. In the main saloon set a *Police Gazette* cover gazed down like a broad wink, while a benign portrait of Booker T. Washington set the tone of bourgeois ambience in the ingenue's home. In the end Micheaux contrived his way around the New York censor board by shifting Robeson from venal preacher to cool detective, at once tricking the audience into expecting a white man's "bad nigger," and symbolically turning away from the hoary stereotype. ⟨. . .⟩

There is no way of knowing whether *Body and Soul* revived the black cinema movement, but it surely arrived coincident with sanguine conditions. By the mid-twenties black communities had become better organized and more self-conscious, and the movies reflected the new awareness. Micheaux not only survived the decade but increased the social thrust of his pictures. His *Spider's Web* (1926) treated the love-hate relationship between the ghetto and the "numbers game"; *The Wages of Sin* (1929) analyzed the strains of urban life upon the black family; *Birthright* (1924) followed a Negro Ivy Leaguer southward to minister to his people's needs. Gradually the translucent watermarks of the middle-class ideologies of personal aspiration and of black solidarity tinged his films.

Thomas Cripps, *Slow Fade to Black: The Negro in American Film, 1900–1942* (New York: Oxford University Press, 1977), pp. 191–93

CHARLES J. FONTENOT, JR.   Hugo M. Gloster writes that in *The Homesteader*, "though indicating the degeneracy of negro life in Southern cities, Micheaux offers no panacea and fails to exhibit the optimism and enterprise which characterize *The Conquest*." This statement indicates a misreading, for while it is true that in *The Conquest* Micheaux does not condemn black urban life to the extent that he does in *The Homesteader* and *The Forged Note*, it is not because he is more optimistic in the earlier novel. Rather, he is investigating a different aspect of the mythology he is trying to construct. The purpose of *The Conquest* is to show that the black race can determine its own destiny, that it can leave behind the moral decadence of cities, and that it can build a more suitable society in the Great Northwest. Speaking through the voice of Oscar Devereaux, Micheaux says: "For years I have felt constrained to deplore the negligence of the colored race in America, in not seizing the opportunity for monopolizing more of the many million acres of rich farm lands in the great Northwest, where immigrants from the old world own many acres of rich farm lands, while the millions of blacks, only a few hundred miles away, are as oblivious to it all as the heathen of Africa are to civilization."

In contrast, *The Forged Note* is Micheaux's attempt to lead the black reader from the decadent world of black urban life to the liberated life of the Great Northwest. He chooses to do this through focusing on the evils existing in black southern life and pointing to some possible reasons for their coming into existence. True, he does not offer a panacea for the problems he exposes, for ready-made solutions are as artificial as the civilization whites have imposed upon blacks. Like Voltaire's Candide, the black race must learn to work toward a realistic goal, not an abstract one such as that described in the ideology of W. E. B. Du Bois. The process of ridding the black race of the weaknesses which prevent natural growth goes through several stages: rejection of interracial marriage, acceptance of moral responsibilities, and embracing education through literature.

> Charles J. Fontenot, Jr., "Oscar Micheaux, Black Novelist and Film Maker," *Vision and Refuge: Essays on the Literature of the Great Plains*, ed. Virginia Faulkner and Frederick C. Luebke (Lincoln: Center for Great Plains Studies/University of Nebraska Press, 1982), pp. 117–18

JOSEPH A. YOUNG   Utilizing the pathos of his own provocative experiences as a Black in early twentieth-century Jim Crow America, Oscar Micheaux fought the cause of individual emancipation by publishing novels that reflect, with minor alterations, the black stereotypes of the post-bellum confederate romanticists: the best of the cavalier racists (Joel Harris and Thomas Page) as well as the worst of the Negrophobes (Thomas Dixon). Micheaux assumed that by adopting the world view of both the proslavery imperialist and the imperialist of industrial expansion, he could escape the humiliating and impotent status typically allotted to the Afro-American and be free to follow the American dream. But such a scheme follows an ambivalent and a dubious line of reasoning. To adopt the world view of the oppressor requires him to reject blackness, that is, to reject both his racial kinsmen and himself. Micheaux, like other black writers of the assimilationist school, idealistically assumed that assimilation of black and white cultures would occur only if Blacks could pass for white; or, if passing for white was a cosmetic impossibility, Blacks could become fit for American culture by adopting Anglo-Saxon myths, Anglo-Saxon values, and Anglo-Saxon philosophy. ⟨. . .⟩

  Most of Micheaux's novels turn on a myth of black inferiority that his black protagonist fancifully transcends. The basic story tells of a conservative Negro who goes to the untamed country, falls in love with a young white woman, and has an imperial dream in which he participates in conquering the wilderness. Because of the laws against miscegenation, he marries instead a young, urban black woman. At first, Micheaux's protagonist is unable to conquer much; in response, he cultivates contempt for urban Blacks, those "bad Negroes" whose chicanery interferes with his own conquests. He loses his first wife, but is able eventually to marry his "dream girl"; he is finally triumphant. ⟨. . .⟩

The importance of Micheaux is not so much in his literary achievements, but in his unwitting illustration of how oppressive myths have been forced on Blacks, especially black novelists who as artists should have been writing in the finest tradition of Western humanism or of a truly black aesthetic philosophy, earnestly attempting to answer the questions, "Who are we?" and "What is life all about?" Addison Gayle in *The Way of the New World* argues that the shortcoming of many black novelists of the past—and even of the present—is in their not having adopted this ideological voice: that the images, metaphors, and symbols that nurture a sense of self-importance and achievement have been created and controlled, manipulated and defined by outsiders. Without this voice or this focus, the mental oppression initiated originally to strip enslaved Africans of their humanity continues.

Micheaux did not address the question, "What is life all about?" Instead, he wrote novels that looked back to the Age of Accommodation and Reconciliation in which Blacks were forced to assume the role of "darky" or "brute," becoming the scapegoat and the butt for the country's frustrations in its attempt to pacify differences between its regional and ethnic white minorities after civil war. Arguably, Micheaux presupposed that the only avenue to success in such a Jim Crow climate would be to use the myth of black inferiority and try to shape it, make it flexible for his personal success. Micheaux became, therefore, an apologist for Booker T. Washington's accommodating strategies and for American imperialism in the hope of gaining material wealth and marginal acceptance. He accepted black folk's position as definitive and as permanently outside or at the bottom of the political, social, and economic mainstream of America. He condemned Blacks to perpetual third-class citizenship, holding them responsible for their condition. And he used the pseudoscience of craniology to dismiss the majority of Blacks as genetically inferior. But Micheaux also suggested that some Blacks could be redeemed if they would follow the teachings and emulate the example of his property-minded, Nietzschean superman hero. If they would migrate west, acquire property, build up capital, and participate in settling the country, this group would in time be saved, or at least be assimilated.

> Joseph A. Young, "Introduction," *Black Novelist as White Racist: The Myth of Black Inferiority in the Novels of Oscar Micheaux* (Westport, CT: Greenwood Press, 1989), pp. ix–xi

◈ Bibliography

The Conquest: The Story of a Negro Pioneer. 1913.

The Forged Note: A Romance of the Darker Races. 1915.

The Homesteader. 1917.

The Wind from Nowhere. 1941.

The Case of Mrs. Wingate. 1944.

The Story of Dorothy Stanfield, Based on a Great Insurance Swindle, and a Woman! 1946.

The Masquerade: An Historical Novel. 1947.

Frank J. Webb
c. 1830–c. 1870

FRANK J. WEBB was probably born sometime in the late 1820s or early 1830s, as the preface by Harriet Beecher Stowe to his only published book, *The Garies and Their Friends* (1857), describes him as a "colored young man, born and reared in the city of Philadelphia." Stowe goes on to describe him as a member of a "large class" in Philadelphia that has "increased in numbers, wealth, and standing," so that they now "constitute a peculiar society of their own, presenting many social peculiarities worthy of interest and attention."

Webb's novel was published in London, and the book is dedicated to Lady Noel Byron, so that it is speculated that Webb resided in England for a time. Webb was also acquainted with Harriet Beecher Stowe and Henry, Lord Brougham, both ardent abolitionists; it may therefore be conjectured that Webb was involved in the abolitionist movement, although this topic does not figure prominently in his novel.

The Garies and Their Friends is the second known novel written by a black American, following William Wells Brown's *Clotel* (1853). It is a pioneering work in being the first black novel to discuss the lives of Northern blacks and to treat with subtlety and depth the idea of the "mixed marriage," a topos that became common in black literature of the later nineteenth and early twentieth centuries. But like many black and white writers of the time, Webb was given to sentimentality, melodrama, and a highly contrived and implausible plot.

The novel focuses on two families, each of whom migrates from the South to the North in the hope of economic betterment but encounter racism in various forms. The Garie family, consisting of a wealthy white man, a mulatto black woman, and their two children, migrate north on the recommendation of Mrs. Garie's cousin, George Winston, a black man who can "pass" for white and who emerges as a trickster figure, revealing his cleverness by bamboozling the white racists he encounters. But the Garie family suffers tragedy when "Slippery" George Stevens, a white man and the villain of the novel, incites a race riot that leads to the death of Mr.

and Mrs. Garie. Meanwhile, the Ellises, an all-black middle-class family
with three children, prosper in spite of the bigotry and violence directed
toward them, and in the end the Ellises' one son, Charlie, marries the
Garies' daughter Emily. Stevens, who has learned that he is a cousin of
Mrs. Garie, commits suicide.

Webb is known to have published two novelettes, "Two Wolves and a
Lamb" (in *New Era*, January–February 1870) and "Marvin Hayle" (in *New
Era*, March–April 1870). Both these works deal with upper-class life in
Europe, and appear to reveal Webb's familiarity with aristocratic society in
London and Paris. These works do not deal significantly with racial issues.

It is not known when Frank J. Webb died, but no further works by him
have come to light. In spite of his obscurity, *The Garies and Their Friends*
remains a landmark work in the history of black American literature, the
model for much that was written in the following half-century.

⬧ *Critical Extracts*

HARRIET BEECHER STOWE   The book which now appears
before the public may be of interest in relation to a question which the
late agitation of the subject of slavery has raised in many thoughtful minds;
viz.—Are the race at present held as slaves capable of freedom, self-govern-
ment, and progress?

The author is a coloured young man, born and reared in the city of
Philadelphia.

This city, standing as it does on the frontier between free and slave
territory, has accumulated naturally a large population of the mixed and
African race.

Being one of the nearest free cities of any considerable size to the slave
territory, it has naturally been a resort of escaping fugitives, or of emancipated
slaves.

In this city they form a large class—have increased in numbers, wealth,
and standing—they constitute a peculiar society of their own, presenting
many social peculiarities worthy of interest and attention.

The representations of their positions as to wealth and education are
reliable, the incidents related are mostly true ones, woven together by a
slight web of fiction.

The scenes of the mob describe incidents of a peculiar stage of excitement, which existed in the city of Philadelphia years ago, when the first agitation of the slavery question developed an intense form of opposition to the free coloured people.

Southern influence at that time stimulated scenes of mob violence in several Northern cities where the discussion was attempted. By prompt, undaunted resistance, however, this spirit was subdued, and the right of free inquiry established; so that discussion of the question, so far from being dangerous in the Free States, is now begun to be allowed in the Slave States; and there are some subjects the mere discussion of which is a half-victory.

The author takes pleasure in recommending this simple and truthfully-told story to the attention and interest of the friends of progress and humanity in England.

> Harriet Beecher Stowe, "Preface," *The Garies and Their Friends* (London: Routledge, 1857), pp. v–vi

ROBERT BONE   *The Garies and Their Friends* (1857), by Frank Webb, has more in common with the protest novels of the 1890's than with the contemporary Abolitionist novels of Brown and Delany. Webb was a member of Philadelphia's free colored population, and he therefore experienced the essential conditions of the middle-class life far in advance of the emancipated freedman. Among these conditions, the freedom to rise is basic. It is reflected in the dominant tone of Webb's novel, which is that of the conventional success story: "The boy that learns to sell matches soon learns to sell other things; he learns to make bargains; he becomes a small trader, then a merchant, then a millionaire." Although he wrote some years before emancipation, Webb was stalking other game than Simon Legree. He is concerned not with slavery but with caste, with the artificial barriers to success which confront the free Negro. He makes a frontal assault on various sectors of the color line, attacking most directly the problems of mixed marriage, and discrimination in employment.

> Robert Bone, *The Negro Novel in America* (New Haven: Yale University Press, 1958; rev. ed. 1965), p. 31

ARTHUR P. DAVIS   Actually Webb is not a strong protest writer. *The Garies and Their Friends* has a tendency to be a "goodwill book." Like Booker T. Washington in *Up from Slavery*, Webb balances the good and the bad white folks so that they neutralize each other. Slippery George is almost a comic book type villain, bad through and through; but his daughter, Lizzie, is an angelic character who urges the dying father to return the money he swindled from the Garie children. Webb depicts a vicious riot scene in which Mr. Ellis is crippled for life, physically and mentally, but he offsets this evil through the kindness of Mr. and Mrs. Burrell, who sound like white patrons of the Urban League. In order to compensate for opportunities denied to Negroes through prejudice, they decide to "make a want" in their business. One also notes that Webb's allusions to abolition are all timid and ambivalent; and more significantly, that there is nowhere in the book a frontal attack on slavery. The one plantation scene, when the Garies leave the South, could have been written by Thomas Nelson Page. Another curious thing is the absence of real anti-slavery persons that Webb could have woven into his plot or at least into the conversation of his characters. From the national scene he could have taken, among other things, David Walker, Douglass, and Garrison; from the local scene, Robert Purvis, James Forten, and Bishop Allen, all well-known Philadelphians and strong civil rights fighters. Was he opposed to the racial approach taken by these leaders? Was he really interested in the anti-slavery fight? We don't know; we do know, however, that the work is not the kind of protest novel that one would expect from an intelligent free Negro in 1875. Perhaps its mildness accounts in some measure for its unpopularity.

With its highly contrived plot, its sharp contrasts of right and wrong, its purple patches, its tear-jerking scenes, its deathbed repentances and near-reconciliations, and its happy endings in marriage for the good of the characters, *The Garies and Their Friends* is typical nineteenth century melodrama, a form which Bone thinks is "a natural vehicle for racial protest." Webb also attempted to instill a bit of humor in the work, but he was not too successful. His major comic figure, Kinch, unlike the comic characters of Brown's works, is a Dickens type rather than a blackface minstrel type. Webb's best example of racial humor is a variant of the "fooling Cap'n Charlie" (the white man) kind. In this case, Negro bellmen in a Philadelphia hotel, all of them members of the Underground Railroad Vigilance Committee, raise funds for their work by "Uncle Tomming" for Southern white guests. They pulled a boner and received a tongue-lashing for their efforts when they put on their act for Mr. Winston, a Negro who was "passing" at the time. The Negro characters in the volume are more convincing on the whole than the white, who tend to be stereotypes. The titular characters, Mr. and Mrs. Garie, somehow never come fully alive. Webb is more successful with Mr. Walters; and whether by accident or by design (I am not quite certain), he created a truly complex and fascinating character (and symbol) in Clarence, the tragic mulatto.

In spite of its several shortcomings, *The Garies and Their Friends* is an exciting and significant novel. Because of its pioneer position and because it foreshadows later important developments in Negro American fiction, it should be much better known.

Arthur P. Davis, "*The Garies and Their Friends*: A Neglected Pioneer Novel," CLA *Journal* 13, No. 1 (September 1969): 33–34

JAMES H. DE VRIES   We may tentatively assume ⟨. . .⟩ that the subject of *The Garies*—Northern racism—was the primary cause of its lack of popularity rather than the use of the conventions of the sentimental novel.

Conversely, one might also assume that the sentimental novel technique enhanced rather than decreased reader interest. Although there are no indications that *The Garies* was ever serialized, some chapters form episodes which leave the reader in suspense until the next chapter. As in most melodramas, the climactic events are elaborately foreshadowed in earlier ones. Furthermore, *The Garies* has its share of melodramatic scenes such as the death of Mrs. Garie as the result of childbirth and exposure to the cold, and the destruction of Mr. Ellis' self-respect when his hands are maimed in the riot. The novel has numerous sentimental partings and reconciliations, and its share of death-bed repentances. Toward the end of the story all the good people, with one exception, are properly rewarded with marriage and good fortune while the villain is suitably punished. The entire plot encourages comparison of the relatively fortunate all-black family, the Ellises, with the ill-fated Garie family, composed of a white Southerner and his mulatto wife and children.

The plot is not necessarily a recapitulation of actual events but may have been constructed to expound upon particular moral issues. As Myron Brightfield indicates, any Victorian who desired factual accounts of social problems could consult other sources. The readers of *The Garies* were reading mainly for pleasure although many probably had philanthropic inclinations. These readers probably needed to be informed in bold outlines of the nature of American racism, and since the readers were already trained to understand and vicariously experience such melodrama, it would be the appropriate vehicle. Also, this melodrama anticipates and accentuates the tragedies of the "good" characters in order to evoke reader sympathy.

Yet there is a tendency for us now to perceive melodrama as reducing moral issues to a simple-minded dichotomy of "good" and "bad" characters. Arthur P. Davis, the only critic to evaluate *The Garies* in some detail, lists its melodramatic characteristics as among the faults of the novel. As Davis observes, *The Garies* does have its share of over-simplified moralization, but actually the melodramatic caricatures communicate complex observations about white racism. In fact, Webb does not construct the characters' personalities strictly according to whether they are prejudiced against blacks. Thus, we find compassionate bigots and inconsiderate abolitionists. Like Dickens, Mrs. Gaskell, and other sentimental writers, Webb believes that good heartedness is the most important, though not the only, ingredient necessary to correct the ills of society. Mrs. Bird befriends Charlie Ellis because their own son had died tragically. Similarly, Mr. Burrell, another color-blind white, later hires Charlie as an apprentice because his wife encourages him to see Charlie as an their own son. "I was trying to imagine, Burrell, how I should feel if you, I, and baby were colored; I was trying to place myself in such a situation. Now we know that our boy, if he is honest and upright— is blest with great talent or genius—may aspire to any station in society that he wishes to obtain." In both the case of Mrs. Bird and the Burrells, filial love binds the black and white in the common goal of raising the next generation.

James H. DeVries, "The Tradition of the Sentimental Novel in *The Garies and Their Friends*," CLA *Journal* 17, No. 2 (December 1973): 242–44

ROBERT E. FLEMING   Frank J. Webb's *The Garies and Their Friends* (1857) deals primarily with middle class characters and so is particularly rich in humorous white characters from this group. For example, Mrs. George Stevens, a social-climbing matron of Philadelphia, calls on her new neighbors. She assumes that they belong to a high social class, for she has already determined that Mr. Garie is a wealthy southerner. What she does not know is that Garie has moved north so that he can live openly with his mulatto wife. Received in a rather dark room one evening, Mrs. Stevens immediately introduces the topic of "niggers" who are ignorant, idle, and incapable of refinement. Having fully displayed her prejudice and lack of refinement, Mrs. Stevens is disconcerted when a lamp is brought into the room and she sees the face of her hostess.

In the same novel, Webb presents a sardonic view of another matron who aspires to social prominence:

For this object [Mrs. Thomas] gave grand dinners and large
evening parties, to which were invited all who, being two
or three removes from the class whose members occupy the
cobbler's bench or the huckster's stall, felt themselves at
liberty to look down upon the rest of the world from the pinnacle
on which they imagined themselves placed. At these social
gatherings the conversation never turned upon pedigree, and if
any of the guests chanced by accident to allude to their
ancestors, they spoke of them as members of the family, who,
at an early period of their lives, were engaged in mercantile
pursuits.

   At such dinners Mrs. Thomas would sit for hours, mumbling
dishes that disagreed with her; smiling at conversations that carried
on in villanous [sic] French, of which language she did not
understand a word; and admiring the manners of addle-
headed young men (who got tipsy at her evening parties), because
they had been to Europe, and were therefore considered
quite men of the world.

Charlie Ellis, a young black servant in the Thomas house, decides to get
himself fired by embarrassing his mistress. First he brings a visiting English
nobleman into Mrs. Thomas's presence when she is wearing a worn old
flannel gown and handkerchief on her head. In spite of his employer's
mortification at being seen in such disarray, Charlie is not fired and must
make further plans.

   While serving at one of Mrs. Thomas's grandest dinners, Charlie snags
her wig with a bent pin and whisks it off as he leaves the room: "The guests
stared and tittered at the grotesque figure she presented,—her head being
covered with short white hair, and her face as red as a peony at the mortifying
situation in which she was placed. As she rose from her chair Charlie
presented himself, and handed her the wig, with an apology for the *accident*.
In her haste to put it on, she turned it wrong side foremost; the laughter
could now no longer be restrained, and in the midst of it Mrs. Thomas left
the room." Webb's use of Charlie to expose the pompousness of Mrs. Thomas
adds a new dimension to the comic situation. Instead of relying on straight-
forward presentation of character and situation to achieve comedy, Webb
introduces a black trickster-figure who perpetrates a joke on the white dupe;
thus, the black reader has the dual pleasure of identifying with the player
of the joke as well as laughing at the victim.

   Robert E. Fleming, "Humor in the Early Black Novel," CLA *Journal* 17, No. 2
(December 1973): 256–57

R. F. BOGARDUS   *The Garies and Their Friends* contains an aspect of black experience that has seldom been treated by history or literature until recent years. And this aspect adds a dimension to Walters' character which not only renders him more complex but examines a layer of black psychology that was usually ignored. This is the presence of the black militant theme, here introduced into the black novel for the first time.

Though more ingredients are necessary, black militance can exist only when anti-white attitudes are clearly expressed by the author. In Webb's novel, they are present—not only in the criticism of white society but in the explicit attitudes expressed by some of the characters. Mrs. Ellis, for example, says to Mrs. Garie, Mr. Garie " 'must love you, Emily, for not one white in a thousand would make such a sacrifice [i.e. marriage] for a colored woman . . . It's real good in him, I declare, and I shall begin to have some faith in white folks after all.' " Besides portraying this open hostility, Webb makes it clear that blacks are " 'Not so aisily bate out—they fight like sevin divils. One o' 'em, night before last, split Mikey Dolan's head clane open, and its a small chance of his life he's got to comfort himself wid.' "

But the most explicitly militant and hostile ingredient of the novel is Walters, who takes no abuse from whites without retaliation. ⟨. . .⟩

⟨. . .⟩ Walters sums up the militant's position: " 'We look belligerent enough, I should think . . . I have asked protection of the law, and it is too weak, or indifferent, to give it; so I have no alternative but to protect myself.' " When they see the fires of the riot in the distance, he urges, " 'we must defend ourselves fully and energetically.' " As the attack on the house begins, Walters commands just as his hero, Toussaint, might have: " 'When we do fire, lét it be to some purpose—let us make sure that someone is hit.' " The battle rages, with the surprised rioters getting the worst of it. First, stones are showered down upon them, and when they resort to guns, bullets are returned—causing many injuries. The rioters respond by trying to knock the door down, but they are bathed in scalding hot water poured on them from an upper window. The temper of the defenders is one of courageous seriousness coupled with exhilaration, and the house and its inhabitants are saved. Through his forceful leadership, Walters has earned a place alongside other prominent black militants.

R. F. Bogardus, "Frank J. Webb's *The Garies and Their Friends*: An Early Black Novelist's Venture into Realism," *Studies in Black Literature* 5, No. 2 (Summer 1974): 18–19

BERNARD W. BELL   Unlike *Clotel*, in *The Garies and Their Friends* we do not find a direct attack on slavery anywhere. Even Webb's allusions to abolition, as critic Arthur P. Davis points out ⟨. . .⟩, are timid and ambivalent. All that literary historians and critics know for certain about Frank Webb is that he was born and reared in Philadelphia. His novel demonstrates, however, that he writes dramatically and persuasively about the problems of growing up as a free black in the City of Brotherly Love and about the tragedy that overcomes an interracial couple who moves North. *The Garies and Their Friends* contrasts the fortunes of two transplanted Southern families. The dark-skinned, lower middle-class Ellises and their three children are contrasted with the interracial Garies: a wealthy white Georgian, his mulatto wife, and their two children. Prejudice and discrimination in jobs, education, housing, public transportation, the media, and public officials culminate in terrorism by Irish immigrants and members of the white working class. By the end of the novel, the Ellis family is crippled but undefeated by the virulence of Northern race prejudice, whereas the Garies, except for young Emily, are completely destroyed by it. The author-narrator's sympathies are clearly with the strivings of black morticians, realtors, and doctors like the Grants and Whistons, who also figure in the narrative.

Instead of Christian charity or black power, Webb's answer to racial discrimination is green power. " 'I tell you what. . . .' " says attorney George Stevens, the bigoted mastermind of the terrorism, " 'If I was a black living in a country like this, I'd sacrifice conscience and everything else to the acquisition of wealth.' " Through success in their small confectionaries, funeral homes, grocery stores, and used clothing shops black characters in the novel strive to achieve power and prestige. They realize that their white contemporaries respected the power of money and property more than democratic and Christian principles. And like Mr. Walters, the "jet-black" millionaire realtor who buys the white hotel in which he is refused dinner in order to evict the offending owner, they are determined that whites will respect their class if not their color. " 'It is impossible,' " says the pragmatic Mr. Walters, " 'to have the same respect for the man who cleans your boots, that you have for the man who plans and builds your house.' " He therefore advises the Ellises to follow the practice of white middle-class families—whose color gives them "incalculable advantage"—and start their son Charlie out selling instead of hiring him out as a servant. ⟨. . .⟩

In contrast to *Clotel*, *The Garies and Their Friends* is more mimetic than historical and more didactic than romantic. The emphasis is on the characters speaking and acting for themselves, and authorial intrusions are limited in the early chapters to descriptions and explanations of character and scene.

After the first twelve chapters the commentary of the omniscient author-narrator, which is generally brief and most obvious at the beginning and ending of the chapters, is used more frequently to establish shifts in time and place, to introduce or reintroduce characters, and to reinforce the themes. The intellectual and moral tone of the author-narrator is consistent with the story, and there is very little distance between the class and racial norms of the implied author and the norms of his apparent white British and American readers.

Bernard W. Bell, *The Afro-American Novel and Its Tradition* (Amherst: University of Massachusetts Press, 1987), pp. 42–44

Bibliography

The Garies and Their Friends. 1857.

Harriet E. Wilson
c. 1828–c. 1863

HARRET E. ADAMS WILSON was born Harriet Adams in 1827 or 1828, as the
U.S. census of 1850, taken on August 24, 1850, gives her age as twenty-two.
On her marriage license her birthplace is given as Milford, New Hampshire.
Nothing is known of her life prior to 1850. Her autobiographical novel,
Our Nig, suggests that she was taken from her home at an early age. The
1850 census lists her as residing with a white family—Samuel Boyles, a
carpenter; his wife, Mary Louisa, and their seventeen-year-old son Charles.
Harriet Adams was probably their indentured servant.

A letter by "Allida" appended to *Our Nig* states that Harriet Adams was
taken to W———, Massachusetts, by an "itinerant colored lecturer" and
that she became a domestic servant at the household of a Mrs. Walker and
was also a straw-hat maker. The itinerant lecturer was probably Thomas
Wilson, listed on his marriage license as a resident or native of Virginia;
he took Harriet Adams back to Milford and married her there on October
6, 1851. The letter by "Allida" reports that the marriage went well at the
beginning, but that the husband soon after ran away to sea. Harriet, already
pregnant, felt obliged to go to the Hillsborough County Farm, a home for
the poor; she gave birth to a son, George Mason Wilson, in May or June
1852.

"Allida" states that the husband then returned and that the family moved
to some town in New Hampshire, where Thomas Wilson supported his
family "decently well." But then Thomas left again, this time for good, and
Harriet, her health failing, put her son in the County Farm; shortly afterward,
however, he was taken into the home of a "kindly gentleman and lady."

The Boston city directory lists a Harriet Wilson, "widow," residing at
various locations in northeastern Boston from 1855 to 1863. "Allida" states
that Wilson's failing health compelled her to write her autobiography as
"another method of procuring her bread." Wilson states in her preface that
she wrote the novel in order to reclaim her son from his foster home. But

George Mason Wilson died of fever on February 15, 1860, at the age of seven years and eight months.

Our Nig; or, Sketches from the Life of a Free Black, although heavily autobiographical, is in fact a novel, probably the first novel published in the United States by a black American. (William Wells Brown's *Clotel* and Frank Webb's *The Garies and Their Friends* precede it, but they were published in England.) *Our Nig* was published anonymously (as "By 'Our Nig' ") but was copyrighted by Harriet E. Wilson and printed for the author on September 5, 1859, by a Boston printing company, George C. Rand & Avery. It tells the story of a white orphan, Mag Smith, who marries a black man named Jim and gives birth to two children. When Jim deserts Mag, she abandons her six-year-old child, Frado, leaving her at the home of a middle-class white family, the Bellmonts. Frado becomes an indentured servant and is brutally treated by Mrs. Bellmont and her daughter Mary, although she develops good relationships with Mr. Bellmont and his son James. At the age of eighteen Frado is able to leave the family and, in spite of ill health and a series of bad jobs, she develops skill as a needleworker. She then meets an itinerant lecturer named Samuel, whom she marries and with whom she has a son. But Samuel abandons her, and the novel ends with Frado fleeing from one town to another to escape slave-catchers and "professed abolitionists" who "didn't want slaves at the South, nor niggers in their own houses, North."

Of the later life of Harriet Wilson nothing is known. The 1860 census lists a Harriet Wilson as a resident in the household of a black couple, Daniel and Susan Jacobs, in Boston; but it gives her age as fifty-two and her birthplace as Fredericksburg, Virginia. It has been conjectured that Wilson deliberately falsified her vital statistics to the census taker in the shadow of the Fugitive Slave Act of 1850. Since she disappears from the Boston city directory after 1863, it is thought that she died then. *Our Nig* was virtually forgotten until Henry Louis Gates, Jr., rediscovered and reprinted it in 1983. It is now regarded as a landmark for being the first novel published in the United States by a black American, the first by a black woman, and a subtle and complex work in its own right.

◈ *Critical Extracts*

HENRY LOUIS GATES, JR.   Wilson's achievement is that she
combines the received conventions of the sentimental novel with certain
key conventions of the slave narratives, then combines the two into *one
new form*, of which *Our Nig* is the unique example. Had subsequent black
authors had this text to draw upon, perhaps the black literary tradition
would have developed more quickly and more resolutely than it did. For
the subtleties of presentation of character are often lost in the fictions of
Wilson's contemporaries, such as Frances E. W. Harper, whose short story
"The Two Offers" was also published in September 1859, and in the works
of her literary "heirs."

Our Nig stands as a "missing link," as it were, between the sustained and
well-developed tradition of black autobiography and the slow emergence of
a distinctive black voice in fiction. That two black women published in
the same month the first novel and short story in the black woman's literary
tradition attests to larger shared cultural presuppositions at work within the
black community than scholars have admitted before. The speaking black
subject emerged on the printed page to declare himself or herself to be a
human being of capacities equal to the whites. Writing, for black authors,
was a mode of being, of self-creation with words. Harriet E. Wilson depicts
this scene of instruction, central to the slave narratives, as the moment
that Frado defies Mrs. Bellmont to hit her. The text reads:

> "Stop!" shouted Frado, "strike me, and I'll never work a mite
> for you;" and throwing down what she had gathered, stood
> like one who feels the stirring of free and independent thoughts.

As had Frederick Douglass in his major battle with overseer Covey, Frado
at last finds a voice with which to define her space. ⟨. . .⟩

In the penultimate chapter of *Our Nig*, the narrator tells us that along
with mastering the needle, Frado learns to master the word:

> Expert with the needle, Frado soon equalled her instructress;
> and she sought to teach her the value of useful books; and while
> one read aloud to the other of deeds historic and names
> renowned, Frado experienced a *new impulse*. She felt herself
> capable of elevation; she felt that this book information supplied
> an *undefined dissatisfaction* she had long felt, but could not
> express. Every leisure moment was carefully applied to self-
> improvement, . . . [emphasis added]

In these final scenes of instruction, Harriet Wilson's text reflects upon its own creation, just as surely as Frado's awakened speaking voice signifies her consciousness of herself as a subject. With the act of speaking alone, Frado assumes a large measure of control over the choices she can possibly make each day. The "free and independent thoughts" she first feels upon speaking are repeated with variation in phrases such as "a new impulse," and "an undefined dissatisfaction," emotions she experiences while learning to read. "This book information," as the narrator tells us, enables Frado to *name things* by reading books. That such an apparently avid reader transformed the salient and tragic details of her life into the stuff of the novel—and was so daring in rendering the structures of fiction—is only one of the wonders of *Our Nig*.

> Henry Louis Gates, Jr., "Introduction," *Our Nig; or, Sketches from the Life of a Free Black* (New York: Random House, 1983), pp. lii–liv

MARGO JEFFERSON   *Our Nig* is part drama, part declaration and part documentary. Wilson sometimes tells her tale baldly; sometimes hurries it along, issuing stage directions and inserting exposition; sometimes crafts it with crisp scenes and dialogue shrewdly attuned to the rhythms and phrasings of class and character. Her tone changes continually—the result, I think, of the haste and pain with which she wrote, the mixed audience she anticipated with dread and the conflict between her gift for biting realism and her taste for genteel lyricism. She will be brusque, then fastidious; she will shift from melancholy to outrage and sarcasm. ⟨. . .⟩

The final chapters are poignant and dissonant. As Frado drags herself from destitution to subsistence and from town to town, "watched by kidnappers, maltreated by professed abolitionists, who didn't want slaves at the South, nor niggers in their own houses, North," the narrator's voice seems about to disappear beneath the weight of its burden. But Wilson draws herself up and abruptly presents a combined autobiographical and fictional ending.

Frado prevails: "Nothing turns her from her steadfast purpose of elevating herself." And, we are told in a tone that fuses a lady's claim to modesty with a free woman's right to privacy, she merits our help—"Enough has been unrolled to demand your sympathy and aid." The closing history of the Bellmonts is briskly supplied. Frado has outlived all but Jane and her husband, who perhaps signify her hopes for a better marriage. Then, in a sweeping Old Testament image, Wilson reduces even them to minor functionaries and elevates Frado to the stature of a chosen prophet and ruler.

Margo Jefferson, "Down & Out & Black in Boston," *Nation*, 28 May 1983, pp. 676–77

IRA BERLIN   Despite its lurid sadism, *Our Nig* is more than an indictment of white racial brutality. While Frado is abused by her mistress, the men of the household—father and sons—provide friendship and protection; indeed, Wilson's account is laced with an undercurrent of unspoken interracial sexuality rarely found in antebellum fiction. To complicate the story further, the protective shield of white manhood is counterposed to the chicanery and deception of a smooth-talking black itinerant who ensures Frado's ruination, marrying, impregnating, and abandoning the friendless young woman and their child. In short, while Wilson places the stock characters of America's interracial drama on stage like so many set pieces, she also adds to the array new characters and thereby provides a more subtle, complex story than most sentimental novels of the day. In many ways, *Our Nig* is more complicated than any black novel before Charles Chesnutt's *The House Behind the Cedars* (1900). Indeed, the questions raised in *Our Nig* about the relation of black men and women in the 19th century and the antebellum black perspective on interracial marriage have hardly been addressed since the novel's publication.

Ira Berlin, "America's First Black Novel," *Washington Post Book World*, 3 July 1983, pp. 1–2

MARILYN RICHARDSON   ⟨. . .⟩ there is ⟨. . .⟩ a certain religious ambiguity ⟨in *Our Nig*⟩. While Frado is clearly a person of strong spiritual leanings, she is, like Sojourner Truth or, later, Frances Harper, quick to recognize the hypocrisy of religious rationales for racial oppression and segregation. She is open to the teachings of the church on some issues, but she is uncertain about spending eternity in a heaven which might also harbor the likes of Mrs. Bellmont who, although a professed Christian, tells her captive servant that "if she did not stop trying to be religious, she would whip her to death."

Frado knows her mistress well. Like Margaret Walker, whose epic novel *Jubilee* gives the lie to every syllable written about black women by Margaret Mitchell, black women writers have, over the years, limned with a deft and unsparing touch the lives, foibles, strengths and weaknesses—warts and all—of those whites against whom they have struggled. In these works, white people are known and understood to their innermost recesses of mind and spirit, while they, in turn, are shown to perceive "their" blacks in terms of the broadest stereotypes and generalizations. That contrast underlies one of the classic recurring symbolic scenes in early black writing, male and female, the confrontation by which the black character claims, once and for all, a distinct sense of self.

There is in *Our Nig* just such a moment of resistance, when Frado finds the strength to stand her ground against Mrs. Bellmont's violence. " 'Stop!' shouted Frado, 'strike me and I'll never work a mite for you'; and throwing down what she had gathered [firewood], stood like one who feels the stirring of free and independent thoughts."

> Marilyn Richardson, "The Shadow of Slavery," *Women's Review of Books* 1, No. 1 (October 1983): 15

BERNARD W. BELL   The point of view, narrative structure, and style ⟨of *Our Nig*⟩ also reveal the double-vision characteristic of the black American experience and the Afro-American novel. Although the story is told primarily by an omniscient, third-person, editorializing narrator, the titles of the first three chapters ("Mag Smith, My Mother," "My Father's Death," and "A New Home for Me") employ the first-person pronoun. The titles of the subsequent eight chapters do not continue this pattern, but the tension in aesthetic distance, suggesting the close identification on all levels of the author-narrator with her protagonist, returns in the opening sentence of chapter 12: "A few years ago, within the compass of my narrative, there appeared often in some of our New England villages, professed fugitives from slavery, who recounted their personal experience in homely phrase, and awakened the indignation of non-slaveholders against brother Pro." The ambivalence and irony here are that Wilson's narrative also recounts her personal experience with "slavery," which she fears will awaken "severe criticism" of her though, as she tells us in the preface, she has "purposely omitted what would most provoke shame in our good anti-slavery friends at home." ⟨. . .⟩

The ambivalence of the author-narrator culminates in the most explicit indictment in the novel of the treatment of blacks in New England by Northern white abolitionists: "Watched by kidnappers, maltreated by professional abolitionists, who didn't want slaves at the South, nor niggers in their own houses, North. Faugh! to lodge one; to eat with one; to admit one through the front door; to sit next one; awful!" This rhetorical strategy of a series of verbal forms, which shift abruptly without quotation marks from the descriptive mode of participial phrases to the dramatic with infinitive phrases enclosed by exclamations, underscores the anomaly of the protagonist's situation and the illuminating power of the author's double vision.

As important to the traditions of the Afro-American novel and feminist literature as the illuminating power of Wilson's double vision and her historical significance is her unique treatment of the theme and character of the tragic mulatto. Harriet Wilson not only introduces into American fiction the first interracial marriage in which the wife is white and husband African, but also develops the character of her mulatto protagonist, the couple's daughter, as an individual rather than a type. Frado's story is not about virtue in distress because of mixed blood and male oppression, but about the violation of human rights because of the hypocrisy of New England Christians and of the racial and class exploitation by some white middle-class women. Also, because Wilson was influenced more by the sophistication and sentimentality of the Euro-American literary tradition than by the Afro-American oral tradition and slave narratives, *Our Nig* clearly and convincingly illustrates that the conventions of both traditions contributed to the development of the early Afro-American novel.

Bernard W. Bell, *The Afro-American Novel and Its Tradition* (Amherst: University of Massachusetts Press, 1987), pp. 48–50

BLYDEN JACKSON   In the treatment of its theme, *Our Nig* disposes contradictorily to what it proposes. Racism undoubtedly was an ugly fact of life for Negroes in the North when *Our Nig* was written. Such racism explained William Wells Brown's ride in a baggage car of a train on which he had anticipated a passenger's reception. It accounted for the antipathy of whites to the spectacle of Frederick Douglass escorting, in no wise as a servant, the white Griffith sisters (who were from England) along a northern street. But Frado's troubles in the Bellmont household hardly seem attributable to her color. Jack Bellmont is her friend. So is his sister Jane and his father's sister, Aunt Abby, while Mr. Bellmont's urbanity toward her never falters. She has problems only with Mrs. Bellmont and Mary, both of whom all who know them regard as cut from the same mold as Cinderella's stepmother. Mr. Bellmont usually walks warily around Mrs. Bellmont, and Mary's schoolmates are overjoyed at any discomfiture to her. Frado has problems with Mrs. Bellmont and Mary not so much becasue she is black as because they are what they are. Moreover, when Frado first goes to school and the children are prepared to be unkind to her, the teacher, Miss Marsh, with commendable tact, so admonishes them that they suspend judgment on Frado until she eventually becomes a favorite with them. The workers on the Bellmont farm ⟨. . .⟩ are as enamored of Frado as her schoolmates. And Aunt Abby's minister experiences no difficulty in conducting himself with Frado according to the higher dictates of his calling.

Indeed, in *Our Nig*, Frado's major source of displeasure seems not to be racistic abuse of herself by others but dissatisfaction with her own color. She wants to be white. She asks James Bellmont, almost as soon as she meets him, why God has made her black and not white. She seeks assurance from others that blacks will go to heaven as well as whites. In her prayers she bemoans her color, always with the implication that she would prefer to be white. Wilson would not be the last black author to debilitate an attack on racism with an unwitting expression of a wish to be white. *Our Nig* illustrates, in one regard at least, racial protest gone awry. Autobiographical in form, it does invite comparison with the slave narrative, which it echoes in form and in such particulars as the helplessness of its protagonist and her ultimate termination of her indenture. And it is a better novel than the first novel written by a black American male. Of Frado and Clotel, Frado is the superior artifact.

Blyden Jackson, *A History of Afro-American Literature* (Baton Rouge: Louisiana State University Press, 1989), Vol. 1, pp. 362–63

CLAUDIA TATE   The lexical identity established between the novel's principal title—*Our Nig*—and its pseudonymous authorial signatory—"Our Nig"—inscribes a sophisticated mode of self-reflexive irony that extenuates direct public censure. The title and the signatory are locked in cyclic parody, like black people in tarface on the minstrel stage; as a result, the aspersion in the self-reflexive title circuitously finds its real target—the very people H. E. W. claimed she wished not to offend in her preface— "our good anti-slavery friends at home." Thus, the text calls attention to the fact that they were ultimately responsible for the quality of life for those free black people who lived among them. In other words, by displacing the well-known slave narrative signatory—Written by Him or Herself—with the diminutive form of a racist epithet—"Our Nig"—the text shifts northern readers' likely resentment of public censure to a deliberately constructed self-derisive humility. Hence, the text exhorts their verification of Frado's hardships and by implication those generally suffered by northern, free, black people by seeing herself from a white perspective. After all, as Wilson insisted with her title, Frado was *their* "nig." Inasmuch as national public opinion had relegated black people, free or slave, to white ownership, Wilson ironically referred to her re-created self as chattel in order to give her voice uncontested authority. As *their* "nig," she could tell her own story of racial abuse seemingly from their point of view and possibly arouse the sympathy of white readers as well as demonstrate that her life was not substantially different from those who were born in bondage. This authorial strategy would also allow her to abort much of the criticism from readers who might regard her story as atypical or exaggerated because technically she was not a slave. However, this epithet may have alienated potential black readers who might not have seen its doubly reflexive irony. The prominent inscription of so hated an epithet among black people may have given them cause to question the racial identity of the book's author, and they may have erroneously concluded that *Our Nig* was a masked white story about black inferiority.

> Claudia Tate, "Allegories of Black Female Desire; or, Rereading Nineteenth-Century Sentimental Narratives of Black Female Authority," *Changing Our Own Words: Essays on Criticism, Theory, and Writing by Black Women*, ed. Cheryl A. Wall (New Brunswick, NJ: Rutgers University Press, 1989), pp. 113–14

BETH MACLAY DORIANI   The novel, like ⟨Harriet⟩ Jacobs's narrative ⟨*Incidents in the Life of a Slave Girl*, 1853⟩, ends with a series of appended letters as do many slave narratives, but Wilson defies the stereotype of the "heroic slave." In her narrative, the writers of the letters—"Allida," Margaret Thorne, and "C. D. S."—do not stop at testifying to the truth of the author's assertions or the goodness of her character. Unlike most slave narratives, these letters have a purpose beyond that of testimony: they appeal to the reader to buy the book, thereby aiding the author in her quest for economic independence. "I hope those who call themselves friends of our dark-skinned brethren," writes Thorne, "will lend a helping hand, and assist our sister not in giving, but in buying a book; the expense is trifling, and the reward of doing good is great." Of course, even at the outset of her narrative Wilson has revised slave narrative conventions by beginning with an account of her parentage, not her own birth. Unlike the "heroic slave," she has a clear and definite knowledge of her heritage and her role in society: she is an individual and not a type. She does not move "up" from slavery or oppression—as in the pattern of ascension that ⟨Robert B.⟩ Stepto describes for Afro-American narrative—but moves "within" the oppressive community, struggling for independence and selfhood within the confines of racism.

Her awareness of this role is most apparent in the way she concludes the novel. The lack of closure, an indicting revision of the white domestic novel, also challenges stereotypes of women. Like Jacobs—and unlike the "tragic mulatta"—she desires financial independence, but the lack of closure at the end of the novel indicates an ambiguity about her own success. Whether she will completely achieve that success depends upon the number of books the people of her racist world will buy. The narrator explicitly appeals to the reader in the novel's closing lines: "[S]he asks your sympathy, gentle reader. Refuse not. . . . Enough has been unrolled to demand your sympathy and aid." It is the poverty and oppression Wilson faces as a black woman that force her to "experiment," first by writing, and then by attempting to sell her story. Her novel lacks closure because her ultimate success is uncertain given the confines of racism. Having no guarantee of a house and home, Wilson must revise the sentimental convention of the happy ending. As an autobiographical act of a black woman, *Our Nig* can end only in uncertainty, if it is to have integrity.

Beth Maclay Doriani, "Black Womanhood in Nineteenth-Century America: Subversion and Self-Construction in Two Women's Autobiographies," *American Quarterly* 43, No. 2 (June 1991): 217–18

◈ Bibliography

Our Nig; or, Sketches from the Life of a Free Black, in a Two-Story White House, North. Showing That Slavery's Shadows Fall Even There. 1859.